The Prepper's Freeze Drying Cookbook

Essential Recipes for Long-Term Survival

G.B. Survival Academy

Table of the Contents:

Introduction

Freeze-drying, also known as lyophilization, is a preservation method that removes moisture from perishable materials, allowing them to be stored for extended periods without refrigeration. The process combines freezing and sublimation to preserve the structure, texture, and nutritional content of the materials, making it particularly advantageous for a variety of applications, from food storage to medical and scientific uses.

The Science of Freeze-drying: An Overview

1. What is Freeze-drying?

Freeze-drying is a dehydration process typically used to preserve perishable items or make materials more convenient for transport. Products that undergo freeze-drying retain their original size and shape, but their weight is significantly reduced due to the removal of water content.

2. The Three Primary Stages:

- **Freezing:** The first step involves freezing the material. It is crucial as it ensures that the moisture content in the material transforms into a solid-state, making the subsequent sublimation process possible.
- **Primary Drying (Sublimation):** During this phase, the frozen water in the material is directly converted into vapor under low pressure without passing through the liquid phase. This direct transition from solid to gas is termed sublimation. By skipping the liquid state, freeze-

drying prevents the structural damage that can be caused by the crystallization of water.

- **Secondary Drying (Desorption):** In this final phase, any remaining moisture, which is typically bound to the material at a molecular level, is removed. The temperature is raised, ensuring the complete removal of water molecules without compromising the integrity of the preserved material.

3. Advantages of Freeze-drying:

Beyond its ability to preserve, freeze-drying offers several other advantages. Foods maintain their shape and color, looking almost as fresh as they did before preservation. Nutritional content remains largely unaffected, making freeze-dried foods just as healthy as their fresh counterparts. Additionally, since the moisture is removed, bacteria, yeast, and mold cannot grow, ensuring the material's longevity.

4. Applications:

While many associate freeze-drying primarily with food preservation – think freeze-dried fruits or astronaut food – its applications are vast. In the pharmaceutical industry, freeze-drying is used to preserve delicate biological materials, including vaccines and other drugs. In the realm of biotechnology and pathology, it's applied to preserve biological specimens. And, of course, in the world of food, it's a method embraced not just for its preservative qualities, but also for the unique textures and flavors it can impart.

Essentials of Freeze-Dried Foods for Survival

In the world of emergency preparedness and survival planning, few resources hold as much importance as food. In dire circumstances, food isn't just about satisfying hunger – it's a lifeline. Among various food preservation methods, freeze-drying stands out, not just for its shelf life but for a myriad of benefits it provides to those prepping for uncertain times.

1. Extended Shelf Life:

The most notable advantage of freeze-dried foods is their extended shelf life. Properly packaged freeze-dried foods can last for 25 to 30 years, ensuring a long-term food solution. This long lifespan means that individuals can store essential foods and not worry about frequent replacements or spoilage.

2. Nutritional Integrity:

Unlike some preservation methods which can degrade the nutritional content of food, freeze-drying retains most of the vitamins and minerals present in fresh food. In emergency scenarios, it's vital not just to consume food, but to intake vital nutrients that maintain health and vitality.

3. Lightness and Portability:

Water is heavy. By removing moisture from food, freeze-drying reduces weight significantly, making these foods highly portable. In situations where mobility is crucial, like evacuations, having lightweight food sources can be a game-changer.

4. Simple Rehydration:

Freeze-dried foods are designed for quick and easy rehydration. By just adding water – either cold or hot – these foods can be returned to their original state, allowing for a near-instant meal. In situations where time and resources are limited, this efficiency can be lifesaving.

5. Taste Preservation:

One might assume that food designed for longevity would compromise on flavor, but freeze-dried foods often retain much of their original taste, ensuring that morale remains high even in challenging times.

6. Versatility in Choices:

From fruits and vegetables to meats and dairy, nearly any food can be freeze-dried. This vast range of options ensures a balanced diet, providing essential macro and micronutrients. In a survival situation, this dietary variety can be essential for maintaining health and well-being.

7. Reduced Dependence on Electricity:

Once food is freeze-dried and packaged, it doesn't require refrigeration. This independence from electricity is crucial, especially in scenarios where power outages are prolonged or where grid access is not available.

8. Waste Minimization:

Freeze-drying can reduce food waste significantly. Foods that might be approaching their freshness limit can be freeze-dried to extend their life, ensuring that resources are maximized and waste is minimized, vital in prolonged emergency situations.

Necessary Equipment for Home Freeze-Drying

As the appeal of preserving food's taste, texture, and nutritional value has grown, so has the interest in home freeze-drying. The process, which once seemed exclusive to laboratories and large manufacturers, is now accessible to everyday consumers. To embark on the journey of home freeze-drying, one must first understand and acquire the necessary equipment. This chapter provides an overview of the fundamental tools required.

1. Home Freeze Dryer:
At the core of the freeze-drying process is the freeze dryer itself. A home freeze dryer is a compact, user-friendly version of its industrial counterpart.

- **Size/Capacity:** Depending on the volume of food you plan to preserve, choose a machine that fits your needs.
- **Vacuum Pump:** Essential for creating the low pressure needed for sublimation. Ensure its durability and ease of maintenance.
- **Control System:** Modern freeze dryers often have digital interfaces, simplifying the process for users.

2. Durable Trays:

Usually made of stainless steel, these trays hold the food inside the freeze dryer. They need to be robust, corrosion-resistant, and easy to clean.

3. Vacuum Sealer:

Post freeze-drying, the food must be sealed in an airtight manner to retain its preservation. A vacuum sealer sucks out the air from the storage bags, ensuring minimal exposure to oxygen.

4. Sealing Bags:

Specifically designed for vacuum sealing, these bags should be puncture-resistant and approved for food storage. Mylar bags are a popular choice due to their durability and ability to block light.

5. Oxygen Absorbers:

These small sachets are added to the sealed bags to capture any residual oxygen. This prevents the oxidation of food, ensuring longer shelf life.

6. Airtight Storage Containers:

For those who opt against bags or need additional protection, airtight containers or food-grade buckets are ideal. These can also be used to store vacuum-sealed bags, offering an added layer of protection against pests or physical damage.

7. Labels and Permanent Markers:

Given the extended shelf life of freeze-dried foods, proper

labeling is crucial. Indicate the food type, freeze-drying date, and any other relevant details.

8. Shelving System:
Organizing your freeze-dried goods in a systematic manner ensures easy access and efficient rotation. A dedicated shelving system, preferably in a cool, dark place, is optimal.

9. Hygrometer:
This device measures humidity. Keeping tabs on moisture levels in your storage area can be crucial in ensuring the longevity of your freeze-dried items.

10. Optional Accessories:
While not essential, items like moisture indicators or silicone mats (for sticky foods) can simplify and optimize the freeze-drying process.

Basic Principles and Techniques

Freeze-drying, or lyophilization as it's scientifically known, is a unique preservation method that removes moisture from materials, ensuring their longevity without compromising their structure, nutritional value, or flavor. By understanding the fundamental principles and techniques, one can appreciate the science and art behind this process.

Steps in the Freeze-Drying Process:

1. Freezing:
This is the foundational step where the material is solidified, and water within it is turned into ice.

- **Importance:** A thorough freeze ensures that the subsequent sublimation process (where ice turns directly into vapor) can occur efficiently.
- **Technique:** The material should be spread out evenly on the trays to promote uniform freezing. Faster freezing rates result in smaller ice crystals, which can lead to a better-quality product.
- **Tip:** Some foods benefit from a slower freezing rate to prevent cellular damage, while others might benefit from quicker rates. Researching specific foods can optimize the quality of the final product.

2. Primary Drying (Sublimation):
Once frozen, the material undergoes the primary drying phase, which accounts for the bulk of the drying process.

- **Importance:** Here, the ice is directly converted into water vapor under reduced pressure, bypassing the liquid phase. This step removes about 95% of the water content from the material.
- **Technique:** The freeze dryer's chamber pressure is reduced (using the vacuum pump), and slight heat is applied to the shelves holding the trays. This encourages the ice to sublimate.

- **Tip:** It's essential to strike a balance in the amount of heat applied. Too much heat can cause melting, while too little can prolong the drying time.

3. Secondary Drying (Desorption):

This phase targets the removal of the residual moisture that might be bound to the material.

- **Importance:** While most of the moisture is removed in the primary drying phase, some water molecules may still be bound to the material. Secondary drying ensures complete dehydration.
- **Technique:** The chamber's temperature is raised higher than in the primary drying phase to break the molecular bonds between the water molecules and the material.
- **Tip:** It's important to monitor this phase closely, as excessive heat can alter the texture or nutritional content of the freeze-dried material.

Tips for Achieving Optimal Results

Freeze-drying is both a science and an art. While the foundational steps of the process remain consistent, there are nuances and tricks that can significantly influence the quality of the end product. Whether you're a novice or an experienced practitioner, these tips can help ensure you achieve the best possible results in your freeze-drying endeavors.

1. Pre-Treatment is Key:

Depending on the type of food, pre-treatment can enhance color, flavor, and texture. For instance:

- Fruits like apples and pears can be soaked in solutions containing ascorbic acid to prevent browning.
- Blanching certain vegetables prior to freeze-drying can help retain their vibrant color.

2. Optimal Slicing:

The thickness of your slices matters. Thinner slices or dices can speed up the drying process, but it's essential not to compromise the food's integrity or nutritional content.

3. Freeze Rapidly:

The quicker the freezing phase, the smaller the ice crystals formed. Smaller crystals typically result in a better final texture. Using pre-frozen foods or ensuring that your freezer is at its coldest setting can help.

4. Avoid Overloading:

While it might be tempting to maximize space, overloading your trays can lead to uneven freeze-drying. Ensure ample space between food items for optimal airflow and sublimation.

5. Regular Maintenance:

Maintain your freeze dryer. Regularly check the vacuum pump oil, keeping it clean. Replace filters as needed and ensure seals are in good condition. A well-maintained machine performs more efficiently and lasts longer.

6. Monitor the Process:

While modern freeze-dryers have automatic settings, it's still beneficial to monitor the process. If you notice ice build-up or any inconsistencies, it might indicate a need to adjust settings or check equipment.

7. Test for Dryness:

Before removing foods, ensure they are entirely dry. You can do this by testing a small piece: it should be brittle and snap easily. If it bends, it might still contain moisture.

8. Store Properly:

Your efforts can be in vain if the freeze-dried products are not stored correctly. Use vacuum-sealed bags, oxygen absorbers, and a cool, dark environment to maximize shelf life.

9. Record Your Experiments:

Different foods may require different settings or pre-treatments. Maintain a logbook of times, temperatures, and outcomes. This can be a valuable reference for future sessions.

10. Stay Informed:

The world of freeze-drying is continuously evolving, with new techniques, equipment, and insights emerging. Join online forums, read relevant literature, and engage with the community to stay updated and improve your skills.

Emergency Storage: Shelf Life and Solutions

In emergency settings, the reliability and longevity of preserved food are paramount. Freeze-drying provides a robust solution, but the way these foods are stored post-process can significantly impact their effectiveness and safety. This chapter delves into best practices for storing freeze-dried foods and considerations for shelf life in high-stakes environments.

1. Packaging Choices Matter:

- **Vacuum-Sealed Bags:** These are the top choice for storing freeze-dried foods. By removing air, they minimize oxidation and microbial growth. Using high-quality, puncture-resistant bags is vital.
- **Mylar Bags:** These offer an additional layer of protection against light, which can degrade the nutritional value of stored foods.
- **Oxygen Absorbers:** Placing these inside sealed bags ensures any residual oxygen is captured, further preventing spoilage and rancidity.

2. Container Storage:

- **Food-Grade Buckets:** Especially useful for larger quantities, these buckets with airtight lids can protect contents from pests, moisture, and physical damage.
- **Desiccants:** These can be placed at the bottom of containers to absorb any inadvertent moisture, ensuring a dry environment.

3. Labeling is Crucial:

Always label stored foods with:

- The type of food.
- Date of freeze-drying.
- Estimated shelf-life. In emergencies, this information helps in prioritizing which foods to consume first and ensures safe consumption.

4. Proper Storage Environment:

- **Cool and Dark:** Extreme temperatures can degrade stored foods faster. A cool, dark place maximizes shelf life.
- **Avoid Moist Areas:** Basements, if damp, can be problematic. Use dehumidifiers if necessary.

5. Rotation System:

Even with extended shelf lives, it's wise to adopt a "first in, first out" system. Regularly rotate stored foods to ensure they're consumed within their optimal time frame.

6. Shelf Life Considerations:

While freeze-drying extends the shelf life dramatically, several factors can influence the actual duration:

- **Type of Food:** High-fat foods may not last as long as leaner counterparts.
- **Storage Conditions:** Fluctuations in temperature, humidity, and exposure to light can reduce shelf life.

- **Packaging Integrity:** Regularly inspect for any signs of package breaches, such as punctures or seal failures.

7. Inspection Before Use:

In emergency scenarios, it's crucial to inspect freeze-dried foods before consumption:

- Check for off-odors or discoloration.
- Ensure packages haven't been compromised.
- Rehydrate a sample; its taste and texture should remain consistent with expectations.

8. Educate and Inform:

In community or group settings, ensure everyone understands the basics of storage, rotation, and consumption. Regular drills or discussions can keep everyone aligned and aware.

Lyophilized Ingredients: A Deep Dive

Fruits: Characteristics, Uses, and Rehydration Techniques

Freeze-drying, or lyophilization, has opened up a world of possibilities for preserving fruits in their near-natural state. By removing moisture under vacuum conditions, we're able to retain the fruit's color, shape, flavor, and most importantly, its nutritional value. This chapter provides a comprehensive look into lyophilized fruits, their unique features, potential uses, and best practices for rehydration.

Characteristics of Lyophilized Fruits:

1. Texture:
Freeze-dried fruits are notably crisp and light, often with a porous structure due to the sublimation of ice directly into vapor, leaving behind tiny cavities.

2. Color:
Unlike many preservation methods, freeze-drying typically retains the vibrant color of fruits. This is because it prevents the browning reactions that often occur in other drying processes.

3. Nutritional Retention:
Vital nutrients, such as vitamins, minerals, and antioxidants, are largely preserved in the freeze-drying process. The cold temperature involved minimizes the degradation of heat-sensitive nutrients.

4. Weight and Volume:
Without water content, freeze-dried fruits are incredibly lightweight, making them advantageous for transport and storage.

5. Shelf Stability:
Due to the absence of moisture and the intact cellular structure, these fruits have an extended shelf life and are less prone to microbial spoilage.

Uses of Lyophilized Fruits:

1. Snacking:
Directly out of the bag, they offer a crunchy, nutritious, and convenient snack.

2. Culinary Creations:
They can be added to dishes like salads, granolas, or desserts for a burst of flavor and texture.

3. Beverages:
When powdered, they serve as a base for smoothies, juices, or even cocktail infusions.

4. Baking:
Their lightweight nature makes them ideal for incorporation into pastries, muffins, or bread without weighing down the mixture.

5. Backpacking and Camping:
Given their weight-to-nutrition ratio, they're a favorite among outdoor enthusiasts.

Rehydration Techniques for Lyophilized Fruits:

1. Cold Water Soaking:
For most fruits, simply soaking them in cold water for 5-15 minutes will rehydrate them. The duration will depend on the fruit's thickness and type.

2. Warm Water Acceleration:

If in a hurry, using warm (not boiling) water can speed up the rehydration process.

3. Direct Incorporation:

In dishes like soups, stews, or oatmeal, adding freeze-dried fruits directly will allow them to rehydrate from the existing moisture.

4. Spritzing:

For applications where only slight rehydration is needed, a spritz or spray of water can be enough.

5. Pulverizing for Powders:

If using the fruits in powdered form, there's no need for rehydration. Grinding freeze-dried fruits into a fine powder allows for their inclusion in drinks, sauces, or as natural food colorings.

Vegetables: Characteristics, Uses, and Rehydration Techniques

Lyophilization, or freeze-drying, stands as a transformative preservation method for vegetables. This technique not only captures the essence of the vegetable's flavor and nutritional profile but also offers extended shelf life and convenience. In this chapter, we will dive deep into the attributes of lyophilized vegetables, their potential applications, and methods to restore their original texture and moisture content.

Characteristics of Lyophilized Vegetables:

1. Texture:
Freeze-dried vegetables possess a crispness that distinguishes them from their dehydrated counterparts. The freeze-drying process leaves behind a light, airy structure that quickly rehydrates when exposed to moisture.

2. Color:
Thanks to the cold environment of freeze-drying, the vibrant colors of vegetables are preserved, making them visually appealing even after extended storage.

3. Nutrient Retention:
Critical vitamins, minerals, and phytonutrients found in vegetables remain largely intact through freeze-drying, ensuring that the preserved products are not just convenient but also nutritious.

4. Weight and Volume:
The removal of water content results in a significant reduction in weight, making freeze-dried vegetables ideal for situations where storage space and transport weight are concerns.

5. Shelf Stability:
Moisture is a primary factor in microbial growth. By eliminating it, freeze-dried vegetables can remain shelf-stable for extended periods, especially when stored in proper conditions.

Uses of Lyophilized Vegetables:

1. Quick Meals:
They can be easily incorporated into dishes like soups, stews, or casseroles, cutting down preparation time.

2. Salad Toppings:
For a unique texture and burst of flavor, sprinkle onto salads directly from the package.

3. Snacking:
When seasoned, certain vegetables like freeze-dried peas or green beans can be a crunchy and healthy alternative to traditional snacks.

4. Backpacking Meals:
Given their lightweight and nutrition density, they are a preferred choice for outdoor enthusiasts and backpackers.

5. Smoothie Boosts:
Powdered freeze-dried vegetables can be added to smoothies for an additional nutritional kick without altering the drink's consistency.

Rehydration Techniques for Lyophilized Vegetables:

1. Soaking in Water:
Placing the vegetables in cold water for 10-30 minutes, depending on their size and type, will typically restore their original texture. Stirring occasionally can speed up the process.

2. Warm Water Method:
Using lukewarm water can expedite the rehydration, especially for denser vegetables like carrots or broccoli.

3. Cooking Directly:
In hot dishes like soups or stir-fries, you can add freeze-dried vegetables directly. They will rehydrate using the moisture from the dish.

4. Steaming:
For vegetables that benefit from a softer texture, steaming after a brief soaking can be effective.

5. Grinding:
For applications that require vegetable powders, such as in sauces, drinks, or as thickening agents, freeze-dried vegetables can be ground into a fine powder without any prior rehydration.

Meats & Proteins: Traits, Uses, and Rehydration

Lyophilization, commonly known as freeze-drying, is a revolutionary preservation method for meats and proteins, ensuring long shelf life without compromising on taste, texture, or nutritional content. This chapter will explore the specifics of freeze-dried meats and proteins, detailing their distinctive attributes, versatile applications, and best practices for bringing them back to their natural state.

Characteristics of Lyophilized Meats and Proteins:

1. Texture:
Once freeze-dried, meats and proteins take on a firm, brittle texture. The removal of moisture through sublimation results in a porous structure that makes rehydration efficient.

2. Color:
The colors of meats and proteins remain relatively consistent after freeze-drying, though they may appear a tad paler compared to their fresh counterparts.

3. Nutrient Retention:
Most of the essential nutrients, including proteins, amino acids, and vitamins, are well-preserved in the freeze-drying process, ensuring that the meat remains a potent source of nutrition.

4. Weight Reduction:
By eliminating moisture, freeze-dried meats and proteins become remarkably lightweight, simplifying storage and transportation concerns.

5. Shelf Stability:
Stored correctly, freeze-dried meats can last for years, making them an optimal choice for long-term storage without the need for refrigeration.

Uses of Lyophilized Meats and Proteins:

1. Emergency Rations:
They're essential for disaster preparedness kits due to their extended shelf life and nutritional content.

2. Camping and Hiking:
Their lightweight nature makes them perfect for backpacking trips where every ounce counts.

3. Quick Meals:
They can be incorporated into dishes like soups, stews, or pasta, offering a protein boost without extended preparation times.

4. Pet Foods:
Freeze-dried meats are also found in high-quality pet foods, prized for their nutritional content and palatability.

5. Snacking:
Some freeze-dried meats, especially seasoned ones, can be eaten directly from the package as a protein-rich snack.

Rehydration Techniques for Lyophilized Meats and Proteins:

1. Cold Water Soak:
Submerging the meat in cold water for 20-60 minutes, depending on the thickness and type, can gradually rehydrate it. It's essential to ensure full immersion and occasionally stir or agitate the water to enhance absorption.

2. Warm Water Acceleration:

For a quicker rehydration, using warm water can reduce the waiting time considerably. This method is especially useful for thin-sliced or diced meats.

3. Cooking Directly:

In recipes that involve ample moisture, like broths or sauces, you can introduce freeze-dried meats directly. They'll absorb the liquid and integrate seamlessly into the dish.

4. Steaming:

For some meats, especially those that benefit from a softer texture, steaming post-soaking can offer optimal results.

5. Rehydration Agents:

For gourmet applications, using broths or flavored liquids instead of water can enhance the taste profile of the rehydrated meat.

Characteristics, Uses, and Rehydration Techniques

The practice of lyophilization, or freeze-drying, extends beyond fruits, vegetables, and meats. It's also an effective preservation method for dairy products and their alternatives. In this chapter, we delve into the specifics of freeze-dried dairy and plant-based alternatives, shedding light on their unique attributes, a multitude of applications, and guidelines for optimal rehydration.

Characteristics of Lyophilized Dairy and Alternatives:

1. Texture:
Once subjected to freeze-drying, dairy products and alternatives develop a crumbly, powdery texture, owing to the removal of moisture.

2. Color:
Generally, freeze-dried dairy and alternatives retain their original color, though they may appear somewhat muted or lighter in shade.

3. Nutrient Retention:
Lyophilization ensures that essential nutrients such as calcium, vitamins, and proteins in dairy and its alternatives remain largely intact.

4. Weight Reduction:
The absence of moisture drastically reduces the weight of the product, making storage and transportation more manageable.

5. Shelf Stability:
When stored in airtight conditions, freeze-dried dairy and alternatives can last for extended periods, often years, without the need for refrigeration.

Uses of Lyophilized Dairy and Alternatives:

1. Emergency Supplies:
Being non-perishable, they're a staple in long-term food storage and emergency preparedness kits.

2. Backpacking and Travel:

Their lightweight and non-refrigeration characteristics make them perfect for on-the-go situations.

3. Baking and Cooking:

From making bread to preparing soups, freeze-dried dairy can be a handy ingredient in various recipes.

4. Beverage Preparation:

Lyophilized milk or plant-based alternatives can be used to prepare beverages, including coffees, teas, or smoothies.

5. Direct Consumption:

Certain products, like freeze-dried yogurts, can be consumed directly as a snack, offering both crunchiness and flavor.

Rehydration Techniques for Lyophilized Dairy and Alternatives:

1. Cold Water Mix:

Gently stirring the freeze-dried product in cold water for a few minutes often suffices, especially for milk and its alternatives.

2. Warm Water Solution:

For products that might need a smoother consistency, like creams or thicker milk alternatives, using warm water can expedite the rehydration process.

3. Direct Addition:

In dishes with ample moisture, you can introduce the freeze-dried dairy directly, allowing it to naturally absorb the surrounding liquids.

4. Blender Integration:

For certain applications like smoothies or shakes, blending the freeze-dried product with other ingredients ensures a smooth consistency.

5. Aromatized Rehydration:

Rehydrating with flavored liquids, like vanilla-infused water for desserts or broth for savory dishes, can add an extra dimension to the reconstituted product.

Herbs and Spices: Characteristics and Uses

Lyophilization, also known as freeze-drying, provides an innovative means of preserving the essence and vitality of herbs and spices. Unlike traditional drying methods, freeze-drying captures the aroma, color, and many nutritional properties of these culinary gems. In this chapter, we will explore the specific attributes of freeze-dried herbs and spices, as well as the myriad of ways they can be used to elevate dishes.

Characteristics of Lyophilized Herbs and Spices:

1. Texture:

Once freeze-dried, herbs and spices become crisp and crumbly, making them easy to crush or grind, yet maintaining a certain lightness.

2. Color:

One of the standout features of the freeze-drying process is its ability to retain the vibrant colors of herbs and spices, in contrast to traditional drying methods that often result in a duller hue.

3. Aroma:

Freeze-dried herbs and spices typically preserve a more potent aroma, closely resembling their fresh counterparts.

4. Flavor Profile:

While the flavor intensity remains, the profile can sometimes be more concentrated, requiring slight adjustments in quantities when used in recipes.

5. Nutrient Retention:

Many of the beneficial compounds, such as antioxidants and essential oils present in herbs and spices, are well-preserved through the lyophilization process.

6. Shelf Stability:

When stored correctly, in a cool, dark place and away from moisture, freeze-dried herbs and spices can have an extended shelf life compared to their traditionally dried counterparts.

Uses of Lyophilized Herbs and Spices:

1. Culinary Dishes:

From soups to stews, stir-fries to salads, they can be incorporated into almost any dish that calls for herbs or spices.

2. Beverage Infusions:

Herbs like mint or chamomile can be used to make aromatic teas or refreshing beverages.

3. Baking:

Spices like cinnamon, nutmeg, or freeze-dried ginger can elevate the flavors in baked goods.

4. Sauces and Dressings:

Blending freeze-dried herbs into sauces or dressings imparts a burst of flavor and vibrant color.

5. Garnishing:

Given their rich colors, they can be used as attractive garnishes on dishes, adding both visual appeal and flavor.

6. Homemade Spice Blends:

Grinding and combining different freeze-dried herbs and spices allows for the creation of personalized seasoning blends.

Emergency Recipes

In critical situations, when time is of the essence and resources may be limited, having a repertoire of quick and nutritious recipes can make a significant difference. Freeze-dried ingredients, with their extended shelf life and nutrient retention, are especially suitable for such scenarios. This section focuses on high-energy recipes crafted for immediate consumption, using lyophilized ingredients to ensure swift preparation without compromising on nutritional value.

Quick Nourishment: High-Energy Recipes for Immediate Consumption

Rapid Rehydration Smoothie:

Ingredients:

- Freeze-dried berries (blueberries, strawberries, raspberries)
- Freeze-dried banana slices
- Freeze-dried yogurt powder
- Water or freeze-dried milk reconstituted

Procedure:
Blend all ingredients until smooth. This concoction provides quick energy, essential vitamins, and probiotics from the yogurt.

Speedy Protein Salad:

Ingredients:

- Freeze-dried chicken or tofu pieces
- Freeze-dried mixed vegetables (bell peppers, carrots, peas)
- Olive oil and freeze-dried herb blend for dressing

Procedure:

Rehydrate chicken or tofu and vegetables briefly in water. Toss with olive oil and herbs. This salad is a protein-packed meal that's ready in minutes.

Instant Energy Trail Mix:

Ingredients:

- Freeze-dried fruits (apple slices, mango chunks, cranberries)
- Nuts (almonds, walnuts, cashews)
- Freeze-dried chocolate bits or cocoa nibs

Procedure:

Combine all ingredients. This mix offers an immediate energy boost, suitable for situations requiring sustained physical exertion.

Swift Soup Solution:

Ingredients:

- Freeze-dried broth cubes or powder
- Freeze-dried vegetable medley
- Freeze-dried meat bits or protein alternatives

Procedure:

Dissolve broth cubes in hot water. Add freeze-dried ingredients and wait a few minutes until everything is rehydrated. This warm soup provides both comfort and necessary nutrients in stressful situations.

Quick Quench Electrolyte Drink:

Ingredients:

- Freeze-dried coconut water powder
- A pinch of salt
- A spoon of freeze-dried honey or agave nectar
- Fresh or purified water

Procedure:

Mix all ingredients in water. This drink ensures hydration and electrolyte balance, vital in emergencies.

Express Energy Bars:

Ingredients:

- Freeze-dried blueberries (1 cup)
- Rolled oats (1 cup)
- Almond butter (½ cup)
- Honey or maple syrup (½ cup)
- Freeze-dried yogurt bites (1 cup)

Procedure:

1. Rehydrate the freeze-dried blueberries by soaking them in a small amount of water for a few minutes. Drain excess water.
2. In a bowl, mix all ingredients until well combined.
3. Press the mixture into a square pan lined with parchment paper.
4. Refrigerate for 1 hour, then cut into bars. Store in a cool place. Ideal for a quick energy boost.

Flash Fuel Peanut Butter Bites:

Ingredients:

- Peanut butter (1 cup)
- Freeze-dried strawberries, powdered (1 cup)

- Chia seeds (½ cup)
- Honey (2 tablespoons)

Procedure:

1. In a mixing bowl, combine all ingredients until well integrated.
2. Roll mixture into small balls. These bites are packed with protein and natural sugars, perfect for an immediate energy lift.

Speedy Oats Revival Bowl:

Ingredients:

- Freeze-dried oats (1 cup)
- Freeze-dried bananas, sliced (½ cup)
- Freeze-dried berries of choice (½ cup)
- Nuts or seeds for crunch (optional)
- Hot water or milk for rehydrating

Procedure:

1. Pour hot water or milk over freeze-dried oats to rehydrate them. Let sit for 3-5 minutes.
2. Add in freeze-dried bananas and berries, allowing them to soak and rehydrate as well.
3. Top with nuts or seeds if desired. This bowl is a hearty, fiber-rich meal that can be prepared in minutes.

Instant Boost Porridge:

Ingredients:

- Freeze-dried quinoa (1 cup)
- Freeze-dried mango chunks (½ cup)
- A pinch of freeze-dried cinnamon powder
- Hot water for rehydrating

Procedure:

1. Rehydrate the freeze-dried quinoa and mango chunks with hot water. Let sit for 5 minutes.
2. Stir in a pinch of freeze-dried cinnamon powder. This porridge offers a good balance of protein, carbohydrates, and natural sugars, essential for quick energy replenishment.

Burst Berry Parfait:

Ingredients:

- Freeze-dried mixed berries (1 cup)
- Freeze-dried Greek yogurt powder (1/2 cup)
- Honey or agave syrup (2 tablespoons)

- Freeze-dried granola (1/2 cup)
- Water for rehydrating

Procedure:

1. Rehydrate the freeze-dried mixed berries with a small amount of water. Let them sit for 5 minutes.
2. In a separate bowl, mix the freeze-dried Greek yogurt powder with water until it reaches a creamy consistency.
3. Layer the rehydrated berries, yogurt, and freeze-dried granola in a glass or bowl. Drizzle with honey or agave syrup. This parfait is a perfect blend of protein, fiber, and natural sugars.

Energizing Nut Butter Spread:

Ingredients:

- Freeze-dried peanut or almond butter powder (1 cup)
- A pinch of freeze-dried cinnamon powder
- Honey or maple syrup (2 tablespoons)
- Water for mixing

Procedure:

1. In a bowl, combine the freeze-dried nut butter powder with a small amount of water until it becomes a spreadable consistency.

2. Mix in the honey or maple syrup and a pinch of freeze-dried cinnamon powder.

3. Spread on whole grain bread or crackers. This spread offers sustained energy from healthy fats and proteins.

Quick Veggie Couscous:

Ingredients:

- Freeze-dried couscous (1 cup)
- Assorted freeze-dried vegetables (carrots, peas, corn) (1 cup)
- Freeze-dried lemon zest (1 teaspoon)
- Olive oil (1 tablespoon)
- Hot water for rehydrating

Procedure:

1. Rehydrate the freeze-dried couscous and vegetables with hot water. Let them sit for 5 minutes.

2. Drizzle with olive oil and sprinkle freeze-dried lemon zest. Stir well. This dish is a quick carbohydrate boost with the added nutrition of vegetables.

Chocolate Energy Balls:

Ingredients:

- Freeze-dried dates (1 cup)
- Freeze-dried cocoa powder (1/4 cup)
- Freeze-dried almond flour (1/2 cup)
- Freeze-dried coconut shreds for coating

Procedure:

1. Rehydrate the freeze-dried dates in a small amount of water for about 10 minutes.
2. In a blender, blend the dates, cocoa powder, and almond flour until they form a sticky mixture.
3. Roll the mixture into small balls and coat with freeze-dried coconut shreds. These energy balls are a tasty, natural sugar boost with added fiber and protein.

Tropical Crunch Mix:

Ingredients:

- Freeze-dried pineapple chunks (1 cup)
- Freeze-dried papaya bits (1 cup)
- Freeze-dried macadamia nuts (1/2 cup)
- Freeze-dried coconut chips (1/2 cup)

Procedure:

1. Mix all the freeze-dried ingredients in a bowl.
2. Consume as is for a quick energy boost. The combination of tropical fruits and nuts provides a delightful and nutritious snack.

Fast-Track Chia Pudding:

Ingredients:

• Freeze-dried chia seeds (1/3 cup)
• Freeze-dried mango chunks (1/2 cup)
• Almond or coconut milk (1 cup)

Procedure:

1. Mix freeze-dried chia seeds with almond or coconut milk. Allow to sit for about 10-15 minutes until a gel-like consistency forms.
2. Rehydrate freeze-dried mango chunks in a small amount of water for 5 minutes.
3. Layer or mix the mango chunks with the chia pudding. This pudding is rich in fiber, antioxidants, and omega-3 fatty acids.

Zesty Lemon Energy Drops:

Ingredients:

- Freeze-dried lemon zest (1 tablespoon)
- Freeze-dried almond flour (1 cup)
- Honey or agave syrup (3 tablespoons)
- Freeze-dried poppy seeds (2 tablespoons)

Procedure:

1. In a bowl, mix the freeze-dried almond flour, honey or agave syrup, freeze-dried lemon zest, and freeze-dried poppy seeds.
2. Roll the mixture into small balls.
3. Consume immediately for a tangy, energizing treat. The combination of lemon and poppy seeds not only offers great flavor but also a quick energy boost.

Instant Savory Yogurt Dip:

Ingredients:

- Freeze-dried Greek yogurt powder (1 cup)
- Freeze-dried dill (1 teaspoon)
- Freeze-dried garlic powder (1/2 teaspoon)
- Water for mixing
- Olive oil (1 tablespoon)

Procedure:

1. Mix the freeze-dried Greek yogurt powder with water until it reaches a creamy consistency.
2. Stir in the freeze-dried dill, garlic powder, and a drizzle of olive oil.
3. Serve with whole grain crackers or rehydrated veggies. This yogurt dip offers a protein-rich snack with the added benefits of herbs and healthy fats.

Berry Bliss Smoothie Bowl:

Ingredients:

- Freeze-dried raspberries (1/2 cup)
- Freeze-dried blackberries (1/2 cup)
- Freeze-dried spinach powder (1 tablespoon)
- Almond milk or water (1 cup)
- Freeze-dried flaxseeds (1 tablespoon)

Procedure:

1. Blend freeze-dried raspberries, blackberries, spinach powder, and almond milk or water until smooth.
2. Pour into a bowl and top with freeze-dried flaxseeds.
3. Consume immediately. This smoothie bowl provides a nutritious blend of fruits, vegetables, and omega-3s for quick nourishment.

Crisp Citrus Bites:

Ingredients:

- Freeze-dried orange segments (1 cup)
- Freeze-dried almonds (1/2 cup)
- Freeze-dried dark chocolate bits (1/3 cup)
- A pinch of freeze-dried sea salt

Procedure:

1. Mix all the freeze-dried ingredients in a bowl.
2. Enjoy as a crunchy snack. The mix of citrus, almonds, and dark chocolate offers a refreshing and energizing combination.

Super Spinach Dip:

Ingredients:

- Freeze-dried spinach powder (1 cup)
- Freeze-dried feta cheese crumbs (1/2 cup)
- Olive oil (2 tablespoons)
- Water for mixing

Procedure:

1. Hydrate the freeze-dried spinach powder with a small amount of water.
2. Once rehydrated, mix with freeze-dried feta cheese crumbs and drizzle with olive oil.
3. Serve immediately with whole grain crackers. This spinach dip combines the goodness of leafy greens and protein-rich feta for an instant energy boost.

Fiesta Bean Mix:

Ingredients:

- Freeze-dried black beans (1 cup)
- Freeze-dried corn kernels (1/2 cup)
- Freeze-dried chili flakes (1 teaspoon)
- Lime zest (from one freeze-dried lime)

Procedure:

1. Mix all freeze-dried ingredients in a bowl.
2. Savor this spicy and tangy mix for an immediate protein-packed snack.

Rapid Raspberry Rolls:

Ingredients:

- Freeze-dried raspberries (1 cup)
- Freeze-dried oat flour (1/2 cup)
- Honey or maple syrup (2 tablespoons)

Procedure:

1. Blend the freeze-dried raspberries in a food processor until they become a powder.
2. In a bowl, mix raspberry powder, oat flour, and honey or maple syrup until a dough forms.
3. Roll into small cylindrical shapes and enjoy. These rolls are an excellent source of fiber and natural sugars.

Instant Walnut Wonder:

Ingredients:

- Freeze-dried walnuts (1 cup)
- Freeze-dried blueberries (1/2 cup)
- Freeze-dried apple bits (1/2 cup)
- A dash of freeze-dried cinnamon

Procedure:

1. Mix all ingredients in a bowl.
2. This combination is rich in omega-3 fatty acids, antioxidants, and dietary fiber.

Turbo Tomato Bruschetta:

Ingredients:

- Freeze-dried tomato chunks (1 cup)
- Freeze-dried basil leaves (1 tablespoon)
- Olive oil (2 tablespoons)
- Garlic powder (1/2 teaspoon)
- Freeze-dried baguette slices

Procedure:

1. Hydrate the freeze-dried tomato chunks and basil leaves in a small amount of water.
2. Once rehydrated, mix tomatoes, basil, olive oil, and garlic powder.
3. Spread over the freeze-dried baguette slices. This is a quick and nutritious appetizer or snack.

Soups

Hearty Vegetable Soup:
Ingredients:

- Freeze-dried carrot slices (1 cup)
- Freeze-dried green beans (1/2 cup)
- Freeze-dried corn kernels (1/2 cup)
- Freeze-dried diced tomatoes (1 cup)
- Freeze-dried basil and oregano (1 teaspoon each)
- Salt and pepper to taste
- Water (4 cups)

Procedure:

1. Add all freeze-dried vegetables to a pot.
2. Add water and bring to a boil.
3. Season with freeze-dried herbs, salt, and pepper.
4. Simmer until all ingredients are rehydrated and flavors meld.

Chicken Noodle Delight:
Ingredients:

- Freeze-dried chicken chunks (1 cup)
- Freeze-dried egg noodles (1 cup)
- Freeze-dried peas (1/2 cup)

- Freeze-dried diced celery (1/2 cup)
- Freeze-dried parsley (1 teaspoon)
- Salt and pepper to taste
- Water (4 cups)

Procedure:

1. Combine freeze-dried chicken, noodles, peas, and celery in a pot.
2. Add water and bring to a boil.
3. Season with freeze-dried parsley, salt, and pepper.
4. Cook until noodles are tender and chicken is rehydrated.

Mushroom and Barley Soup:

Ingredients:

- Freeze-dried mushroom slices (1 cup)
- Freeze-dried pearl barley (1/2 cup)
- Freeze-dried diced onions (1/4 cup)
- Freeze-dried thyme (1 teaspoon)
- Salt and pepper to taste
- Water (4 cups)

Procedure:

1. In a pot, combine freeze-dried mushrooms, barley, and onions.

2. Add water and start to heat.

3. Season with freeze-dried thyme, salt, and pepper.

4. Let simmer until barley is soft and mushrooms are fully rehydrated.

Spicy Lentil Soup:

Ingredients:

- Freeze-dried lentils (1 cup)
- Freeze-dried diced tomatoes (1 cup)
- Freeze-dried chopped spinach (1/2 cup)
- Freeze-dried chili flakes (1 teaspoon)
- Freeze-dried cumin (1/2 teaspoon)
- Salt to taste
- Water (4 cups)

Procedure:

1. Place freeze-dried lentils, tomatoes, and spinach in a pot.

2. Add water and bring to a simmer.

3. Season with freeze-dried chili flakes, cumin, and salt.

4. Continue to simmer until lentils are tender.

Thai-inspired Coconut Soup:

Ingredients:

- Freeze-dried coconut milk powder (1 cup)
- Freeze-dried shrimp or tofu chunks (1/2 cup)
- Freeze-dried bell peppers, sliced (1/2 cup)
- Freeze-dried lemon grass (1 stalk, pounded)
- Freeze-dried lime leaves (3-4)
- Freeze-dried chili flakes (to taste)
- Water (3 cups)

Procedure:

1. Dissolve the coconut milk powder in water in a pot.
2. Add freeze-dried shrimp or tofu, bell peppers, lemon grass, and lime leaves.
3. Bring to a boil and then let simmer.
4. Season with freeze-dried chili flakes.
5. Cook until all ingredients are rehydrated and the soup is aromatic.

Southwestern Bean Soup:

Ingredients:

- Freeze-dried black beans (1 cup)
- Freeze-dried corn kernels (1/2 cup)
- Freeze-dried diced tomatoes (1 cup)
- Freeze-dried jalapeno slices (1 tablespoon, or to taste)

- Freeze-dried cumin (1 teaspoon)
- Salt and pepper to taste
- Water (4 cups)

Procedure:

1. Combine freeze-dried black beans, corn, tomatoes, and jalapenos in a pot.
2. Pour in water and bring to a boil.
3. Season with freeze-dried cumin, salt, and pepper.
4. Simmer until beans are soft and all ingredients are fully rehydrated.

Minestrone Soup:

Ingredients:

- Freeze-dried pasta (1/2 cup)
- Freeze-dried kidney beans (1/2 cup)
- Freeze-dried zucchini slices (1/2 cup)
- Freeze-dried spinach (1/4 cup)
- Freeze-dried basil and oregano (1 teaspoon each)
- Freeze-dried diced tomatoes (1 cup)
- Salt and pepper to taste
- Water (4 cups)

Procedure:

1. In a pot, add freeze-dried pasta, kidney beans, zucchini, spinach, and diced tomatoes.
2. Pour in water and start to heat.
3. Season with freeze-dried basil, oregano, salt, and pepper.
4. Boil until pasta is al dente and vegetables are tender.

Russian Borscht:

Ingredients:

- Freeze-dried beet slices (1 cup)
- Freeze-dried cabbage shreds (1/2 cup)
- Freeze-dried diced potatoes (1/2 cup)
- Freeze-dried dill (1 teaspoon)
- Freeze-dried garlic (1/2 teaspoon)
- Salt and pepper to taste
- Water (4 cups)
- Lemon juice or vinegar for acidity (to taste)

Procedure:

1. In a pot, combine freeze-dried beet slices, cabbage, and potatoes.
2. Add water and bring to a boil.
3. Season with freeze-dried dill, garlic, salt, and pepper.
4. Continue to simmer until all ingredients are rehydrated.

5. Adjust acidity with lemon juice or vinegar as desired.

Creamy Potato and Leek Soup:

Ingredients:

- Freeze-dried diced potatoes (1 cup)
- Freeze-dried leek slices (1/2 cup)
- Freeze-dried parsley (1 teaspoon)
- Salt and pepper to taste
- Freeze-dried cream powder (1/4 cup)
- Water (4 cups)

Procedure:

1. Mix freeze-dried diced potatoes and leek slices in a pot.
2. Add water and bring to a simmer.
3. Season with freeze-dried parsley, salt, and pepper.
4. Once potatoes and leeks are rehydrated, add the cream powder and stir until dissolved.

Soothing Pumpkin Soup:

Ingredients:

- Freeze-dried pumpkin powder (1 cup)
- Freeze-dried ginger (1/2 teaspoon)
- Freeze-dried nutmeg (a pinch)
- Salt to taste
- Water (3 cups)

Procedure:

1. Dissolve freeze-dried pumpkin powder in water in a pot.
2. Heat the mixture and bring to a boil.
3. Season with freeze-dried ginger, nutmeg, and salt.
4. Continue to simmer until soup thickens and flavors meld.

Tomato Basil Bliss:

Ingredients:

- Freeze-dried tomato powder (1 cup)
- Freeze-dried basil leaves (1 tablespoon)
- Freeze-dried garlic powder (1/2 teaspoon)
- Salt and pepper to taste
- Water (4 cups)

Procedure:

1. Mix freeze-dried tomato powder with water in a pot.
2. Heat the mixture, bringing it to a gentle boil.
3. Add freeze-dried basil and garlic powder.
4. Simmer until fully rehydrated and flavors meld. Season with salt and pepper.

Curried Chickpea Soup:

Ingredients:

- Freeze-dried chickpeas (1 cup)
- Freeze-dried curry powder (1 tablespoon)
- Freeze-dried diced carrots (1/2 cup)
- Freeze-dried onion flakes (1/4 cup)
- Salt to taste
- Water (4 cups)

Procedure:

1. Add freeze-dried chickpeas, carrots, and onion flakes to a pot.
2. Pour in water and heat.
3. Once boiling, season with freeze-dried curry powder and salt.
4. Simmer until chickpeas are tender and flavors have combined.

Asian-Inspired Miso Soup:

Ingredients:

- Freeze-dried miso paste powder (2 tablespoons)
- Freeze-dried tofu cubes (1/2 cup)
- Freeze-dried seaweed (1/4 cup)
- Freeze-dried spring onion slices (1/4 cup)
- Water (4 cups)

Procedure:

1. Dissolve freeze-dried miso paste powder in water in a pot.
2. Add freeze-dried tofu cubes and seaweed.
3. Heat gently, making sure not to boil to preserve the miso's nutrients.
4. Once warm and ingredients are rehydrated, garnish with spring onion slices.

Tuscan White Bean Soup:

Ingredients:

- Freeze-dried cannellini beans (1 cup)
- Freeze-dried rosemary (1 teaspoon)

- Freeze-dried garlic flakes (1/2 teaspoon)
- Freeze-dried diced tomatoes (1/2 cup)
- Salt and pepper to taste
- Water (4 cups)

Procedure:

1. Add freeze-dried cannellini beans and tomatoes to a pot.
2. Cover with water and begin to heat.
3. Season with freeze-dried rosemary, garlic flakes, salt, and pepper.
4. Simmer until beans are tender and flavors have melded.

Seafood Chowder:

Ingredients:

- Freeze-dried shrimp and fish pieces (1 cup total)
- Freeze-dried potato dices (1/2 cup)
- Freeze-dried sweetcorn kernels (1/4 cup)
- Freeze-dried cream powder (1/4 cup)
- Salt and pepper to taste
- Water (4 cups)

Procedure:

1. In a pot, add freeze-dried shrimp, fish, potato dices, and sweetcorn.

2. Pour in water and bring to a boil.
3. Once boiling, reduce to a simmer and add the cream powder.
4. Stir until dissolved and continue to simmer until seafood is tender and flavors combined.

Moroccan Chickpea and Lentil Soup:

Ingredients:

- Freeze-dried chickpeas (1/2 cup)
- Freeze-dried lentils (1/2 cup)
- Freeze-dried diced tomatoes (1 cup)
- Freeze-dried ground cumin (1 teaspoon)
- Freeze-dried paprika (1/2 teaspoon)
- Water (5 cups)
- Salt to taste

Procedure:

1. Combine freeze-dried chickpeas, lentils, and tomatoes in a pot.
2. Add water and bring to a boil.
3. Stir in freeze-dried cumin and paprika.
4. Reduce heat and simmer until lentils and chickpeas are tender.

Creamy Spinach and Artichoke Soup:

Ingredients:

- Freeze-dried spinach (1 cup)
- Freeze-dried artichoke hearts (1/2 cup)
- Freeze-dried cream powder (1/2 cup)
- Water (4 cups)
- Salt and pepper to taste

Procedure:

1. Add water to a pot and bring to a simmer.
2. Mix in freeze-dried spinach and artichoke hearts.
3. Once rehydrated, add freeze-dried cream powder and mix until smooth.
4. Season with salt and pepper.

Beef and Vegetable Medley:

Ingredients:

- Freeze-dried beef cubes (1 cup)
- Freeze-dried mixed vegetables (carrots, peas, green beans - 1 cup total)
- Freeze-dried beef broth powder (1 tablespoon)
- Water (5 cups)
- Salt and pepper to taste

Procedure:

1. Add freeze-dried beef and vegetables to a pot.
2. Mix in water and heat to a boil.
3. Stir in freeze-dried beef broth powder.
4. Reduce heat and simmer until beef is tender.

Roasted Red Pepper and Tomato Soup:

Ingredients:

- Freeze-dried roasted red pepper powder (1 cup)
- Freeze-dried tomato powder (1/2 cup)
- Freeze-dried basil (1 teaspoon)
- Water (4 cups)
- Salt to taste

Procedure:

1. Mix freeze-dried roasted red pepper and tomato powder in a pot with water.
2. Heat the mixture to a boil.
3. Stir in freeze-dried basil and simmer for a few minutes.
4. Season with salt.

Garlic and Herb Broth:

Ingredients:

- Freeze-dried garlic flakes (1 tablespoon)
- Freeze-dried mixed herbs (basil, oregano, rosemary - 1 tablespoon total)
- Freeze-dried vegetable broth powder (1 tablespoon)
- Water (4 cups)

Procedure:

1. Add water to a pot and bring to a simmer.
2. Stir in freeze-dried garlic flakes, mixed herbs, and vegetable broth powder.
3. Let the broth simmer for several minutes to meld flavors.

Sweet Potato and Curry Soup:

Ingredients:

- Freeze-dried sweet potato powder (1 cup)
- Freeze-dried curry powder (1 teaspoon)
- Water (4 cups)
- Salt to taste

Procedure:

1. Dissolve freeze-dried sweet potato powder in water in a pot.
2. Heat and bring to a gentle boil.
3. Stir in freeze-dried curry powder and season with salt.
4. Simmer until flavors are well combined.

Broccoli and Cheddar Soup:

Ingredients:

- Freeze-dried broccoli florets (1 cup)
- Freeze-dried cheddar cheese powder (1/2 cup)
- Freeze-dried onion powder (1 teaspoon)
- Water (4 cups)
- Salt and pepper to taste

Procedure:

1. Add water to a pot and bring to a boil.
2. Add in freeze-dried broccoli florets and simmer until rehydrated.
3. Mix in freeze-dried cheddar cheese powder and onion powder.
4. Season with salt and pepper, and simmer until all ingredients are well combined.

Zucchini Basil Cream Soup:

Ingredients:

- Freeze-dried zucchini slices (1 cup)
- Freeze-dried basil leaves (1 tablespoon)
- Freeze-dried cream powder (1/4 cup)
- Water (4 cups)
- Salt to taste

Procedure:

1. Bring water to a boil in a pot.
2. Add freeze-dried zucchini slices and simmer until tender.
3. Stir in freeze-dried basil leaves and cream powder.
4. Season with salt and let it simmer for a few more minutes.

Goulash Soup:

Ingredients:

- Freeze-dried beef cubes (1 cup)
- Freeze-dried bell peppers, mixed colors (1/2 cup)
- Freeze-dried onion slices (1/4 cup)
- Freeze-dried paprika (1 teaspoon)

- Water (5 cups)
- Salt and pepper to taste

Procedure:

1. Add water to a pot and bring to a boil.
2. Add in freeze-dried beef cubes, bell peppers, and onions.
3. Season with freeze-dried paprika, salt, and pepper.
4. Simmer until beef is tender and flavors meld.

Corn and Green Chili Soup:

Ingredients:

- Freeze-dried corn kernels (1 cup)
- Freeze-dried green chili flakes (1 tablespoon)
- Freeze-dried onion powder (1/2 teaspoon)
- Water (4 cups)
- Salt to taste

Procedure:

1. In a pot, bring water to a boil.
2. Mix in freeze-dried corn kernels, green chili flakes, and onion powder.
3. Season with salt and let it simmer until corn is rehydrated and flavors are well combined.

Caramelized Onion and Gruyère Soup:

Ingredients:

- Freeze-dried onion slices (1 cup)
- Freeze-dried Gruyère cheese powder (1/4 cup)
- Freeze-dried vegetable broth powder (1 tablespoon)
- Water (4 cups)
- Salt and pepper to taste

Procedure:

1. Dissolve vegetable broth powder in water and bring to a boil in a pot.
2. Add freeze-dried onion slices and simmer until tender.
3. Mix in Gruyère cheese powder and season with salt and pepper.
4. Simmer for a few more minutes until flavors meld.

Pea and Ham Soup:

Ingredients:

- Freeze-dried green peas (1 cup)
- Freeze-dried ham dices (1/2 cup)
- Freeze-dried mint leaves (1 teaspoon)
- Water (4 cups)
- Salt and pepper to taste

Procedure:

1. Bring water to a boil in a pot.
2. Add in freeze-dried green peas and ham.
3. Season with freeze-dried mint leaves, salt, and pepper.
4. Simmer until peas are soft and flavors combine.

Vegetarian Dishes

Creamy Broccoli and Cheese Soup:

Ingredients:

- Freeze-dried broccoli florets
- Freeze-dried cheddar cheese powder
- Freeze-dried onion slices
- A pinch of nutmeg
- Salt and pepper to taste
- Fresh or purified water

Procedure:

Rehydrate the broccoli and onion in water. In a pot, bring the water to boil and add the rehydrated ingredients. Simmer for 10 minutes. Mix in the cheddar cheese powder, stirring continuously. Season with nutmeg, salt, and pepper. Serve hot.

Veggie Risotto Medley:

Ingredients:

- Freeze-dried arborio rice
- Mix of freeze-dried vegetables (peas, bell peppers, carrots)

- Freeze-dried parmesan cheese powder
- Olive oil
- Salt and herbs to taste
- Fresh or purified water

Procedure:

Start by rehydrating the rice and vegetables. In a pan, heat a bit of olive oil and add the rehydrated rice and vegetables. Fry lightly. Gradually add water and stir continuously. As the rice gets cooked and creamy, add the parmesan cheese powder. Season with salt and herbs. Serve warm.

Spinach and Feta Casserole:

Ingredients:

- Freeze-dried spinach leaves
- Freeze-dried feta cheese crumbles
- Freeze-dried tomatoes
- Olive oil
- Salt, pepper, and herbs to taste
- Fresh or purified water

Procedure:

Rehydrate the spinach, tomatoes, and feta cheese. In a baking dish, mix the rehydrated ingredients. Drizzle with olive oil and season with salt, pepper, and herbs. Bake in a makeshift oven or heat source until the top is golden brown. Serve hot.

Quinoa and Vegetable Pilaf:

Ingredients:

- Freeze-dried quinoa grains
- Mix of freeze-dried vegetables (zucchini, corn, beans)
- Freeze-dried lemon zest
- Olive oil
- Salt and herbs to taste
- Fresh or purified water

Procedure:

Rehydrate the quinoa and vegetables. In a pot, heat a bit of olive oil, then add the rehydrated ingredients. Add water and cook until quinoa is fluffy. Mix in the lemon zest and season with salt and herbs. Serve warm.

Lentil and Vegetable Curry:

Ingredients:

- Freeze-dried lentils
- Freeze-dried vegetable mix (cauliflower, potato, carrots)
- Freeze-dried curry spice mix
- Coconut oil or ghee
- Salt to taste
- Fresh or purified water

Procedure:

Rehydrate the lentils and vegetables. In a pot, heat the oil or ghee, and add the curry spice mix. Once fragrant, add the rehydrated lentils and vegetables. Pour in the water and let it simmer until lentils are cooked and vegetables are tender. Season with salt. Serve with rice or on its own.

Stuffed Bell Peppers:

Ingredients:

- Freeze-dried bell peppers
- Freeze-dried quinoa or rice grains
- Freeze-dried black beans
- Freeze-dried corn kernels
- Freeze-dried tomato slices

- Freeze-dried cheese (like cheddar or mozzarella)
- Spices: cumin, paprika, and salt to taste
- Fresh or purified water

Procedure:

Rehydrate the bell peppers, quinoa or rice, beans, corn, tomatoes, and cheese. In a separate bowl, mix quinoa or rice, black beans, corn, tomatoes, spices, and half of the cheese. Stuff this mixture into the bell peppers. Sprinkle the remaining cheese on top. Place the stuffed peppers in a pot with a little water and cover. Cook over a heat source until the peppers are tender and the cheese is melted. Serve hot.

Chickpea and Spinach Stew:

Ingredients:

- Freeze-dried chickpeas
- Freeze-dried spinach leaves
- Freeze-dried onion slices
- Freeze-dried garlic granules
- Freeze-dried tomato chunks
- Olive oil
- Spices: cumin, coriander, and salt to taste
- Fresh or purified water

Procedure:

Rehydrate the chickpeas, spinach, onion, garlic, and tomatoes. In a pot, heat the olive oil and sauté the onions and garlic. Once fragrant, add the chickpeas, spinach, tomatoes, and spices. Add enough water to cover and simmer until chickpeas are tender. Adjust the seasoning before serving. Best served warm with bread or rice.

Vegetarian Shepherd's Pie:

Ingredients:

- Freeze-dried lentils
- Mixed freeze-dried vegetables (peas, carrots, corn, green beans)
- Freeze-dried mashed potato flakes
- Freeze-dried onion slices
- Olive oil
- Herbs: rosemary, thyme, and salt to taste
- Fresh or purified water

Procedure:

Rehydrate the lentils, vegetables, mashed potato flakes, and onions. In a pan, sauté the onions in olive oil until translucent. Add the rehydrated lentils and vegetables, season with herbs, and simmer with a little water until well-combined and aromatic. In a separate pot, prepare the mashed potatoes using the potato flakes and water. Place the lentil and vegetable mixture in a dish, and top with the mashed potatoes, smoothing the top. Heat over a fire or heat source until the top is slightly crispy. Serve warm.

Cauliflower and Pea Curry:

Ingredients:

- Freeze-dried cauliflower florets
- Freeze-dried green peas
- Freeze-dried curry spice mix
- Freeze-dried onion slices
- Freeze-dried garlic granules
- Coconut oil or ghee
- Salt to taste
- Fresh or purified water

Procedure:

Rehydrate the cauliflower, peas, onion, and garlic. In a pot, heat the oil or ghee, then add the onions and garlic. When translucent, stir in the curry spice mix until aromatic. Add the cauliflower and peas, mixing to coat them with the spices. Pour in enough water to cover and let it simmer until cauliflower is tender and the flavors meld together. Season with salt and serve with rice or flatbread.

Mediterranean Couscous Salad:

Ingredients:

- Freeze-dried couscous grains
- Freeze-dried cherry tomatoes
- Freeze-dried cucumber slices
- Freeze-dried black olives
- Freeze-dried feta cheese crumbles
- Olive oil
- Lemon juice or freeze-dried lemon powder
- Herbs: dried oregano, salt, and pepper to taste
- Fresh or purified water

Procedure:

Rehydrate the couscous, tomatoes, cucumber, olives, and feta. In a large bowl, toss together the rehydrated ingredients. In a separate bowl, mix olive oil, lemon juice (or rehydrated lemon powder), oregano, salt, and pepper. Pour this dressing over the couscous mixture and toss well. Let sit for a few minutes to allow flavors to meld. Serve cold or at room temperature.

Tofu and Vegetable Stir-Fry:

Ingredients:

- Freeze-dried tofu cubes
- Mixed freeze-dried vegetables (bell peppers, broccoli, snap peas, carrots)
- Freeze-dried soy sauce or tamari powder
- Freeze-dried ginger slices
- Freeze-dried garlic granules
- Sesame oil
- Fresh or purified water

Procedure:

Rehydrate the tofu, vegetables, ginger, and garlic. In a pan or wok, heat the sesame oil and add the ginger and garlic. Once aromatic, add the vegetables and tofu. Stir-fry for a few minutes. Mix in the rehydrated soy sauce or tamari and continue to stir-fry until vegetables are tender but still have a bite. Serve with rice or noodles.

Hearty Veggie Stew:

Ingredients:

- Mixed freeze-dried vegetables (potatoes, carrots, peas, green beans, celery)
- Freeze-dried tomato chunks
- Freeze-dried onion slices
- Herbs: dried thyme, rosemary, bay leaf, salt, and pepper to taste
- Olive oil
- Fresh or purified water

Procedure:

Rehydrate the vegetables, tomatoes, and onions. In a large pot, heat olive oil and sauté the onions until translucent. Add the rehydrated vegetables and tomatoes. Add enough water to cover and toss in the herbs. Simmer until the vegetables are tender and flavors are well combined. Adjust seasoning as needed. Remove bay leaf before serving. Serve with bread or over rice.

Eggplant Parmesan Layers:

Ingredients:

- Freeze-dried eggplant slices
- Freeze-dried tomato sauce powder
- Freeze-dried mozzarella cheese crumbles
- Freeze-dried Parmesan cheese powder
- Herbs: dried basil, oregano, and salt to taste
- Olive oil
- Fresh or purified water

Procedure:

Rehydrate the eggplant slices, tomato sauce, mozzarella, and Parmesan. In a pot, combine the tomato sauce powder with water to make a sauce. Season with basil, oregano, and salt. In a separate pan, lightly fry the eggplant slices in olive oil until golden on each side. In a dish, layer the fried eggplant slices, tomato sauce, mozzarella, and a sprinkle of Parmesan. Repeat layers until all ingredients are used. Place the dish over a heat source and cook until the cheese melts and the dish is heated through. Serve warm.

Zucchini and Tomato Casserole:

Ingredients:

- Freeze-dried zucchini slices
- Freeze-dried tomato slices
- Freeze-dried onion rings
- Grated freeze-dried Parmesan cheese
- Herbs: dried basil, oregano, and salt to taste
- Olive oil
- Fresh or purified water

Procedure:

Rehydrate the zucchini, tomatoes, and onions. In a casserole dish, layer zucchini slices, followed by tomatoes and onions. Sprinkle with a bit of basil, oregano, salt, and grated Parmesan. Repeat layers until all ingredients are used. Drizzle with olive oil. Cook until vegetables are tender and cheese is melted. Serve warm.

Vegetable and Bean Chili:

Ingredients:

- Mixed freeze-dried vegetables (bell peppers, corn, onions)
- Freeze-dried kidney beans

- Freeze-dried tomato sauce powder
- Chili powder, cumin, paprika, and salt to taste
- Olive oil
- Fresh or purified water

Procedure:

Rehydrate the vegetables, beans, and tomato sauce. In a pot, heat olive oil and sauté the rehydrated onions until translucent. Add other vegetables, beans, and rehydrated tomato sauce. Season with chili powder, cumin, paprika, and salt. Let simmer until flavors meld and chili thickens. Serve warm with rice or bread.

Pesto Pasta Salad:

Ingredients:

- Freeze-dried pasta (like fusilli or penne)
- Freeze-dried basil leaves
- Freeze-dried garlic granules
- Freeze-dried pine nuts or walnuts
- Grated freeze-dried Parmesan cheese
- Olive oil
- Salt and black pepper to taste
- Fresh or purified water

Procedure:

Rehydrate pasta until al dente. In a blender or mortar and pestle, combine rehydrated basil leaves, garlic, nuts, grated Parmesan, olive oil, salt, and pepper. Blend until a pesto sauce forms. Toss the rehydrated pasta with the pesto. Serve chilled or at room temperature.

Vegetable and Cheese Omelette:

Ingredients:

- Freeze-dried eggs (usually in powdered form)
- Freeze-dried bell peppers
- Freeze-dried mushrooms
- Grated freeze-dried cheddar cheese
- Herbs: dried chives, salt, and pepper to taste
- Butter or oil for frying
- Fresh or purified water

Procedure:

Rehydrate the egg powder, bell peppers, mushrooms, and cheese. In a bowl, whisk the rehydrated egg powder with chives, salt, and pepper. Heat butter or oil in a frying pan. Pour the egg mixture and spread the rehydrated bell peppers and mushrooms evenly. Once the bottom is set, sprinkle the cheese on one half and fold the omelette over. Continue cooking until cheese melts. Serve warm.

Potato Gnocchi with Herb Sauce:

Ingredients:

- Freeze-dried potato flakes
- Freeze-dried basil leaves
- Freeze-dried garlic granules
- Freeze-dried pine nuts or almonds
- Grated freeze-dried Parmesan cheese
- Olive oil
- Salt to taste
- Fresh or purified water

Procedure:

Rehydrate potato flakes and form into small gnocchi shapes. Boil until they float to the surface. In a blender or mortar and pestle, blend rehydrated basil, garlic, nuts, Parmesan, olive oil, and salt until a smooth sauce forms. Toss the gnocchi in the herb sauce and serve warm.

Vegetarian Paella:

Ingredients:

- Freeze-dried rice
- Mixed freeze-dried vegetables (bell peppers, green beans, peas)
- Freeze-dried saffron threads
- Paprika, salt, and black pepper to taste
- Olive oil
- Fresh or purified water

Procedure:

Rehydrate the rice and vegetables. In a large pan, heat olive oil and sauté the vegetables. Add rice, rehydrated saffron, paprika, salt, and water. Cook until rice is tender and has absorbed the water. Adjust seasoning and serve warm.

Sweet Potato and Black Bean Bowl:

Ingredients:

- Freeze-dried sweet potatoes
- Freeze-dried black beans
- Freeze-dried corn kernels
- Freeze-dried cilantro leaves
- Lime juice powder

- Chili powder, cumin, salt, and black pepper to taste
- Olive oil
- Fresh or purified water

Procedure:

Rehydrate sweet potatoes, black beans, corn, and cilantro. In a bowl, combine the rehydrated ingredients with chili powder, cumin, rehydrated lime juice, olive oil, salt, and pepper. Mix well and serve either warm or at room temperature.

Ratatouille with Polenta:

Ingredients:

- Freeze-dried eggplant slices
- Freeze-dried zucchini slices
- Freeze-dried bell peppers
- Freeze-dried tomatoes
- Freeze-dried polenta or cornmeal
- Herbs: dried basil, oregano, and thyme
- Olive oil
- Salt and black pepper to taste
- Fresh or purified water

Procedure:

Rehydrate the vegetables. In a pan, heat olive oil and sauté the vegetables with basil, oregano, and thyme until tender. In a separate pot, cook the rehydrated polenta or cornmeal until thick and creamy, seasoning with salt and pepper. Serve the ratatouille over the polenta.

Curried Cauliflower Rice:

Ingredients:

- Freeze-dried cauliflower rice
- Freeze-dried peas and carrots mix
- Curry powder, turmeric, and cumin to taste
- Freeze-dried cilantro leaves for garnish
- Olive oil or coconut oil
- Salt and black pepper to taste
- Fresh or purified water

Procedure:

Rehydrate cauliflower rice and the peas and carrots mix. In a pan, heat oil and add the spices, stirring until fragrant. Add the rehydrated ingredients and sauté until heated through. Garnish with rehydrated cilantro leaves before serving.

Butternut Squash and Sage Risotto:

Ingredients:

- Freeze-dried butternut squash cubes
- Freeze-dried arborio rice
- Freeze-dried sage leaves
- Grated freeze-dried Parmesan cheese
- Olive oil
- Salt and black pepper to taste
- Fresh or purified water

Procedure:

Rehydrate the butternut squash cubes and arborio rice. In a pan, heat olive oil and sauté rehydrated rice until translucent. Gradually add water, stirring continuously until the rice is creamy. Add rehydrated butternut squash cubes, sage, and season with salt and pepper. Top with rehydrated Parmesan cheese before serving.

Green Pea and Mint Soup:

Ingredients:

- Freeze-dried green peas
- Freeze-dried mint leaves
- Onion powder and garlic powder to taste

- Olive oil
- Salt and black pepper to taste
- Fresh or purified water

Procedure:

Rehydrate the green peas and mint leaves. In a pan, heat olive oil and sauté onion and garlic powder until fragrant. Add the rehydrated peas, mint, and enough water to cover. Simmer until peas are tender. Blend until smooth, season with salt and pepper, and serve warm.

Three-Bean Salad:

Ingredients:

- Freeze-dried kidney beans
- Freeze-dried black beans
- Freeze-dried chickpeas
- Freeze-dried corn kernels
- Freeze-dried red bell pepper bits
- Lime juice powder
- Chili powder, cumin, salt, and black pepper to taste
- Olive oil

Procedure:

Rehydrate beans, corn, and red bell pepper. In a large bowl, mix together all rehydrated ingredients. Sprinkle lime juice powder, chili powder, cumin, salt, and pepper. Drizzle with olive oil, mix well, and serve chilled or at room temperature.

Stir-fried Tempeh with Veggies:

Ingredients:

- Freeze-dried tempeh cubes
- Mixed freeze-dried vegetables (bell peppers, snow peas, carrots)
- Soy sauce or tamari powder
- Sesame oil
- Fresh or purified water

Procedure:

Rehydrate tempeh cubes and vegetables. In a wok or large pan, heat sesame oil and stir-fry the rehydrated tempeh until golden. Add the vegetables and continue stir-frying until tender. Sprinkle soy sauce or tamari powder, mix well, and serve hot.

Caramelized Onion and Mushroom Tart:

Ingredients:

- Freeze-dried onion slices
- Freeze-dried mushroom slices
- Freeze-dried thyme leaves

- Olive oil or butter
- Salt and black pepper to taste
- Ready-made tart crust or freeze-dried tart crust

Procedure:

Rehydrate the onion and mushroom slices. In a pan, heat the olive oil or butter and sauté the onions until they start to caramelize. Add the mushrooms and cook until tender. Sprinkle with thyme, salt, and pepper. Fill the ready-made tart crust with the mixture and bake until golden.

Vegetable Lasagna:

Ingredients:

- Freeze-dried lasagna sheets
- Mixed freeze-dried vegetables (zucchini, bell peppers, spinach)
- Freeze-dried ricotta cheese
- Freeze-dried mozzarella cheese
- Tomato sauce powder or freeze-dried tomato sauce
- Salt, black pepper, and Italian seasoning to taste

Procedure:

Rehydrate lasagna sheets, vegetables, and cheeses. Layer a baking dish with a small amount of rehydrated tomato sauce. Place a layer of lasagna sheets, then vegetables, ricotta, mozzarella, and tomato sauce. Repeat layers until all ingredients are used up, finishing with mozzarella on top. Season with salt, pepper, and Italian seasoning. Bake until bubbly and golden.

Mushroom and Spinach Frittata:

Ingredients:

- Freeze-dried mushroom slices
- Freeze-dried spinach leaves
- Freeze-dried whole eggs
- Freeze-dried feta cheese (optional)
- Olive oil
- Salt and black pepper to taste
- Fresh or purified water

Procedure:

Rehydrate the mushroom slices, spinach leaves, and feta cheese. In a bowl, rehydrate and whisk the eggs, adding salt and pepper. Heat olive oil in a pan, add mushrooms and spinach, and sauté until tender. Pour the eggs over the vegetables, sprinkle with feta, and cook until set. Place under a broiler for a few minutes to brown the top if desired.

Vegetable Pot Pie:

Ingredients:

- Mixed freeze-dried vegetables (peas, carrots, corn, green beans)
- Freeze-dried white sauce or gravy powder
- Salt and black pepper to taste
- Freeze-dried pie crust or ready-made pie crust

Procedure:

Rehydrate the mixed vegetables. Prepare the white sauce or gravy as per instructions. Mix the vegetables with the sauce or gravy, seasoning with salt and pepper. Fill a pie dish with the mixture, and cover with rehydrated pie crust. Bake until the crust is golden and the filling is bubbly.

Sundried Tomato and Olive Pasta:

Ingredients:

- Freeze-dried pasta of choice
- Freeze-dried sundried tomatoes
- Freeze-dried black olives
- Freeze-dried basil leaves
- Olive oil, salt, and black pepper to taste
- Fresh or purified water

Procedure:

Rehydrate pasta, sundried tomatoes, black olives, and basil leaves. In a pan, heat olive oil, add the tomatoes and olives, and sauté for a few minutes. Toss in the rehydrated pasta and mix well. Season with salt, pepper, and basil leaves. Serve immediately.

Main Courses: Nutrient

In emergency situations or when long-lasting, nutrient-packed meals are needed, main courses play a vital role. Leveraging the properties of freeze-dried ingredients, these recipes provide both dense nutrition and the flavorsome experience of a hearty meal, ensuring that individuals are well-fed and energized.

Hearty Vegetable Stew:

Ingredients:

- Freeze-dried mixed vegetables (carrots, peas, beans, broccoli)
- Freeze-dried potato dices
- Freeze-dried beef or vegetable broth cubes
- Herbs and spices as preferred (like freeze-dried garlic, rosemary, thyme)

Procedure:

Rehydrate the freeze-dried ingredients in warm water. In a pot, bring the broth to a boil, add the vegetables, herbs, and spices, and let simmer until flavors meld. Serve warm.

Protein-Packed Rice Pilaf:

Ingredients:

- Freeze-dried rice
- Freeze-dried chicken chunks or lentils for a vegetarian version
- Freeze-dried bell peppers and peas
- Freeze-dried onion flakes and garlic powder

Procedure:

Rehydrate all the ingredients. In a pot, sauté the onions and garlic, add the rice, protein source, and double the amount of water. Cook until rice is fluffy. Stir in vegetables and serve.

Quick-fix Pasta Marinara:

Ingredients:

- Freeze-dried pasta
- Freeze-dried tomato sauce powder

- Freeze-dried ground beef or mushroom slices for a vegetarian twist
- Italian herb blend and freeze-dried Parmesan cheese

Procedure:

Rehydrate the freeze-dried components. Boil the pasta until al dente. In another pan, cook the meat or mushrooms, add the tomato sauce and herbs, and simmer. Combine with pasta and top with cheese.

Savory Bean Chili:

Ingredients:

- Freeze-dried kidney beans or black beans
- Freeze-dried diced tomatoes
- Freeze-dried ground turkey or tofu crumbles
- Chili spice mix

Procedure:

Rehydrate the beans, tomatoes, and protein source. In a pot, combine all ingredients, add the spice mix, and let simmer until thickened and flavors combine.

Wholesome Shepherd's Pie:

Ingredients:

- Freeze-dried ground beef or lentils
- Freeze-dried mixed vegetables (corn, peas, carrots)
- Freeze-dried mashed potato flakes
- Freeze-dried gravy mix

Procedure:

Rehydrate and cook the beef or lentils. Layer in a baking dish, followed by the vegetables. Prepare the mashed potatoes and spread them on top. Bake until the top is golden. Serve with gravy.

Portable Snacks

Whether you're in an emergency, on a long hike, or simply in need of quick energy during a busy day, portable snacks are invaluable. With freeze-dried ingredients at the helm, these recipes guarantee prolonged shelf life, nutrient density, and flavor, all packed into convenient, ready-to-eat forms.

Tropical Fruit Medley:

Ingredients:

- Freeze-dried slices of mango, pineapple, and papaya
- Coconut flakes

Procedure:

Simply mix the rehydrated fruit slices and coconut flakes in a bag. This fruit medley offers quick sugars for instant energy and tropical flavors for a refreshing bite.

Protein Crunch Bars:

Ingredients:

- Freeze-dried peanut or almond butter
- Freeze-dried oats
- Freeze-dried berries (like blueberries or cranberries)
- Honey or maple syrup

Procedure:

Mix rehydrated nut butter, oats, and berries. Drizzle in honey or syrup to bind. Press into a tray, freeze until set, and cut into bars.

Veggie Crisps:

Ingredients:

- Freeze-dried slices of beetroot, zucchini, and carrot
- Sea salt or seasoning of choice

Procedure:

Rehydrate the vegetable slices briefly to retain some crispness. Season and enjoy as a crunchy, nutritious alternative to chips.

Nut and Seed Trail Mix:

Ingredients:

- Freeze-dried nuts (almonds, walnuts, cashews)
- Freeze-dried seeds (pumpkin, sunflower)
- Freeze-dried chocolate bits or dried fruit for sweetness

Procedure:

Combine all ingredients in a bag. This mix is a dense source of energy, perfect for sustained activities.

Cheesy Kale Chips:

Ingredients:

- Freeze-dried kale leaves
- Freeze-dried cheese powder (like cheddar or parmesan)
- Olive oil spray
- Seasoning of choice

Procedure:

Lightly spray rehydrated kale leaves with olive oil. Sprinkle with rehydrated cheese powder and seasoning. Bake until crispy or enjoy as is for a softer texture.

Savory Protein Bites:

Ingredients:

- Freeze-dried chickpeas or lentils
- Freeze-dried herbs (like rosemary or thyme)
- Olive oil and sea salt

Procedure:

Rehydrate chickpeas or lentils, mix with herbs, olive oil, and salt. Bake until crunchy or enjoy as a softer, protein-packed snack.

Rehydration Solutions and Beverages

Staying hydrated is paramount, especially in emergency or strenuous situations. While water is the primary source of hydration, sometimes, especially during physical exertion or in hot environments, the body needs more than just water. Electrolytes and certain nutrients become essential. This chapter delves into recipes for rehydration solutions and beverages crafted with freeze-dried ingredients to ensure quick preparation and optimal hydration.

Basic Electrolyte Drink:

Ingredients:

- Freeze-dried coconut water powder
- A pinch of sea salt
- A spoon of freeze-dried honey or agave nectar
- Fresh or purified water

Procedure:

Mix all ingredients in water. This drink ensures hydration and maintains electrolyte balance, essential in physically demanding scenarios.

Herbal Hydration Tea:

Ingredients:

- Freeze-dried herbal tea blend (like chamomile, peppermint, hibiscus)
- Freeze-dried lemon slices or lemon powder
- Water

Procedure:

Steep the rehydrated tea blend and lemon in hot water. This soothing beverage aids in relaxation and gentle hydration.

Energizing Berry Boost:

Ingredients:

- Freeze-dried berry mix (like blueberries, raspberries, strawberries)
- Freeze-dried green tea powder
- A touch of freeze-dried honey or stevia for sweetness

Procedure:

Blend rehydrated berries with water, mix in the green tea powder, and sweeten as desired. This beverage provides antioxidants and a mild caffeine kick for energy.

Recovery Citrus Quencher:

Ingredients:

- Freeze-dried orange and lime slices
- A pinch of sea salt
- A spoon of freeze-dried honey or maple syrup
- Sparkling or still water

Procedure:

Mix all ingredients in water, ensuring a balance of sweetness and tanginess. This drink is especially refreshing post-workout or after sun exposure.

Nutrient-Rich Vegetable Broth:

Ingredients:

- Freeze-dried vegetable broth cubes or powder
- Freeze-dried mixed vegetables (like celery, carrots, onion)
- Herbs and spices as desired

Procedure:

Dissolve broth cubes in hot water. Add rehydrated vegetables and herbs, and let simmer briefly. This warm beverage offers both hydration and nourishment, perfect for colder environments or when feeling under the weather.

Creamy Nut Milkshake:

Ingredients:

- Freeze-dried almond or cashew powder
- Freeze-dried banana slices
- A touch of vanilla extract
- Water or ice cubes

Procedure:

Blend all ingredients until smooth. This rich and creamy drink provides hydration alongside healthy fats and proteins, great for replenishing energy.

Cold Environment Meals

In cold environments, where the body expends more energy to maintain its core temperature, the need for warm, hearty meals becomes even more pronounced. These recipes, crafted with freeze-dried ingredients, ensure that individuals facing cold climates receive not just sustenance but also the comfort of a hot meal, helping to combat the chill and replenish spent energy.

Classic Chicken Soup:

Ingredients:

- Freeze-dried chicken chunks
- Freeze-dried mixed vegetables (carrots, celery, onions)
- Freeze-dried chicken broth cubes or powder
- Freeze-dried noodles or rice
- Herbs like thyme and parsley

Procedure:
Rehydrate all ingredients. In a pot, simmer chicken and vegetables in broth until tender, add noodles or rice and herbs, and cook until done. Serve steaming hot.

Hearty Beef and Barley Stew:

Ingredients:

- Freeze-dried beef cubes
- Freeze-dried pearl barley
- Freeze-dried mixed root vegetables (potatoes, carrots, turnips)
- Beef broth or vegetable broth
- Bay leaf and rosemary

Procedure:

Rehydrate the ingredients. In a pot, brown beef cubes, add vegetables, barley, broth, and herbs, and simmer until everything is tender and flavors meld.

Spicy Lentil and Vegetable Curry:

Ingredients:

- Freeze-dried lentils
- Freeze-dried mixed vegetables (like bell peppers, peas, cauliflower)
- Freeze-dried coconut milk powder
- Curry spices and freeze-dried garlic and ginger

Procedure:

Rehydrate the lentils and vegetables. Sauté spices, garlic, and ginger, add vegetables and lentils, stir in coconut milk, and simmer until aromatic and flavorsome.

Rustic Potato and Leek Soup:

Ingredients:

- Freeze-dried potato flakes or dices
- Freeze-dried leek slices
- Vegetable or chicken broth
- Herbs like dill or chives

Procedure:

Rehydrate potatoes and leeks. In a pot, simmer them in broth until tender. Blend to desired consistency, and stir in herbs before serving.

Creamy Mushroom Risotto:

Ingredients:

- Freeze-dried risotto rice
- Freeze-dried assorted mushrooms
- Freeze-dried chicken or vegetable broth
- Freeze-dried Parmesan cheese
- Freeze-dried garlic and onion flakes

Procedure:

Rehydrate mushrooms, garlic, and onion. Sauté them, add risotto rice, gradually pour in broth while stirring continuously. Once cooked and creamy, sprinkle with Parmesan cheese.

Spaghetti Bolognese:

Ingredients:

- Freeze-dried spaghetti
- Freeze-dried ground beef
- Freeze-dried tomato sauce powder
- Italian herbs and freeze-dried garlic

Procedure:

Rehydrate beef and tomato sauce. Sauté beef, add herbs, garlic, and sauce. Cook until flavors develop. Serve over rehydrated and cooked spaghetti.

Savory Pumpkin and Bean Chili:

Ingredients:

- Freeze-dried black beans
- Freeze-dried pumpkin chunks
- Freeze-dried diced tomatoes
- Chili spices, cumin, and freeze-dried garlic
- Optional toppings: Freeze-dried grated cheese, sour cream

Procedure:

Rehydrate beans, pumpkin, and tomatoes. Sauté spices and garlic, add beans, pumpkin, and tomatoes, and simmer until flavors meld and the pumpkin is tender. Serve hot with optional toppings.

Hearty Sausage and Vegetable Casserole:

Ingredients:

- Freeze-dried sausage slices
- Freeze-dried mixed vegetables (like green beans, broccoli, bell peppers)
- Freeze-dried potato dices
- Freeze-dried beef or chicken broth
- Herbs like sage and rosemary

Procedure:

Rehydrate the ingredients. In a pot or casserole dish, combine sausage, vegetables, potatoes, broth, and herbs. Bake or simmer until everything is tender and flavors merge.

Quinoa and Roasted Red Pepper Soup:

Ingredients:

- Freeze-dried quinoa
- Freeze-dried roasted red pepper slices
- Freeze-dried vegetable or chicken broth
- Freeze-dried garlic and onion flakes
- Smoked paprika and cumin

Procedure:

Rehydrate peppers, garlic, and onion. Sauté them, add spices, quinoa, and broth, and simmer until quinoa is cooked and the soup is aromatic.

Creamy Salmon and Dill Chowder:

Ingredients:

- Freeze-dried salmon chunks
- Freeze-dried potato dices
- Freeze-dried corn kernels
- Freeze-dried cream or coconut milk powder
- Dill and freeze-dried lemon slices

Procedure:

Rehydrate salmon, potatoes, and corn. In a pot, simmer salmon, potatoes, and corn in water or broth. When almost done, stir in rehydrated cream or coconut milk, dill, and lemon. Cook until flavors combine.

Tomato and Lentil Stew:

Ingredients:

- Freeze-dried green or brown lentils
- Freeze-dried diced tomatoes
- Freeze-dried spinach or kale
- Italian herbs, freeze-dried garlic, and bay leaf
- Optional: Freeze-dried feta or Parmesan cheese for topping

Procedure:

Rehydrate lentils, tomatoes, and greens. In a pot, simmer lentils and tomatoes with herbs, garlic, and bay leaf. Once lentils are tender, stir in greens and cook briefly. Serve with optional cheese sprinkled on top.

Wild Rice and Mushroom Pilaf:

Ingredients:

- Freeze-dried wild rice
- Freeze-dried mixed mushrooms (like shiitake, porcini, button)
- Freeze-dried chicken or vegetable broth
- Thyme and freeze-dried garlic flakes

Procedure:

Rehydrate mushrooms and garlic. Sauté them briefly, add wild rice, and stir in broth. Cook until rice is tender and flavors infuse.

Sweet Potato and Chickpea Curry:

Ingredients:

- Freeze-dried sweet potato chunks
- Freeze-dried chickpeas
- Freeze-dried coconut milk powder
- Curry spices, turmeric, and freeze-dried garlic
- Fresh cilantro for garnish (optional)

Procedure:

Rehydrate sweet potatoes, chickpeas, and coconut milk. In a pot, sauté garlic and spices, add sweet potatoes and chickpeas, followed by coconut milk. Simmer until everything is tender. Garnish with cilantro if available.

Lamb and Rosemary Stew:

Ingredients:

- Freeze-dried lamb cubes
- Freeze-dried diced carrots and parsnips
- Freeze-dried lamb or beef broth
- Rosemary, thyme, and freeze-dried garlic flakes

Procedure:

Rehydrate lamb, vegetables, and broth. Brown lamb cubes in a pot, add vegetables, broth, and herbs. Simmer until meat is tender and flavors have melded.

Three Bean and Kale Soup:

Ingredients:

- Freeze-dried red beans, black beans, and white beans
- Freeze-dried kale or collard greens
- Freeze-dried vegetable or chicken broth
- Cumin, paprika, and freeze-dried onion flakes

Procedure:

Rehydrate beans, kale, and broth. In a pot, sauté onion and spices, add beans, kale, and broth, and simmer until beans are tender and the soup is flavorful.

Creamy Pesto and Sun-dried Tomato Pasta:

Ingredients:

- Freeze-dried pasta of choice
- Freeze-dried basil pesto powder
- Freeze-dried sun-dried tomatoes
- Freeze-dried cream powder or cheese for added richness

Procedure:

Cook rehydrated pasta. In a separate pot, rehydrate pesto, tomatoes, and cream or cheese. Combine with cooked pasta, stir well, and serve hot.

Spinach and Feta Pie:

Ingredients:

- Freeze-dried spinach leaves
- Freeze-dried feta cheese crumbles
- Freeze-dried phyllo dough or alternative
- Nutmeg, pepper, and freeze-dried onion slices

Procedure:

Rehydrate spinach, feta, and phyllo. Sauté onion, add spinach, season with nutmeg and pepper. Layer phyllo in a baking dish, spread the spinach mixture, sprinkle feta on top, and cover with more phyllo. Bake until golden brown.

Beef and Vegetable Pot Pie:

Ingredients:

- Freeze-dried beef chunks
- Freeze-dried mixed vegetables (peas, carrots, green beans)
- Freeze-dried beef broth and roux (flour+butter) for thickening
- Freeze-dried pie crust or dough

Procedure:

Rehydrate beef, vegetables, broth, and dough. In a pot, simmer beef and vegetables in broth until tender. Thicken with roux. Pour into a baking dish, cover with dough, and bake until crust is golden.

Barley and Roasted Vegetable Soup:

Ingredients:

- Freeze-dried barley grains
- Freeze-dried roasted vegetable mix (zucchini, bell peppers, eggplant)
- Freeze-dried vegetable broth
- Thyme, rosemary, and freeze-dried garlic flakes

Procedure:

Rehydrate barley, vegetables, and broth. In a pot, combine all ingredients, simmer until barley is tender and vegetables have infused their roasted flavor into the soup.

Mushroom and Thyme Risotto:

Ingredients:

- Freeze-dried Arborio rice
- Freeze-dried assorted mushrooms
- Freeze-dried vegetable or chicken broth
- Thyme, freeze-dried onion, and Parmesan cheese for garnish

Procedure:

Rehydrate mushrooms and broth. Sauté onion in a pan, add mushrooms, rice, and gradually ladle in broth, stirring continuously until rice is tender and creamy. Finish with a sprinkle of Parmesan cheese.

Lentil and Bacon Stew:

Ingredients:

- Freeze-dried green lentils
- Freeze-dried bacon bits
- Freeze-dried diced tomatoes
- Bay leaf, paprika, and freeze-dried garlic slices

Procedure:

Rehydrate lentils, bacon, and tomatoes. In a pot, fry bacon bits until crispy, add garlic, lentils, tomatoes, and spices. Simmer until lentils are tender and flavors meld.

Pea and Ham Soup:

Ingredients:

- Freeze-dried split peas
- Freeze-dried ham chunks
- Freeze-dried vegetable broth
- Freeze-dried onion flakes and bay leaf

Procedure:

Rehydrate peas, ham, and broth. In a pot, combine all ingredients and simmer until peas are soft and the soup has thickened. Remove bay leaf before serving.

Cauliflower and Cheese Casserole:

Ingredients:

- Freeze-dried cauliflower florets
- Freeze-dried cheese sauce powder
- Optional toppings: breadcrumbs and freeze-dried chives

Procedure:

Rehydrate cauliflower and cheese sauce. In a baking dish, layer cauliflower, pour cheese sauce over, sprinkle with breadcrumbs, and bake until golden brown and bubbly. Garnish with chives.

Potato and Leek Gratin:

Ingredients:

- Freeze-dried potato slices
- Freeze-dried leek slices
- Freeze-dried cream or milk powder
- Thyme, freeze-dried garlic slices, and grated cheese for topping

Procedure:

Rehydrate potatoes, leeks, and cream/milk. Layer potatoes and leeks in a baking dish, season with thyme and garlic, pour rehydrated cream/milk over, top with cheese, and bake until golden and the potatoes are tender.

Freeze-Dried Sweet Treats

Freeze-Dried Strawberry Crumble:

Ingredients:

- 1 cup freeze-dried strawberries
- 1/2 cup granulated sugar
- 3/4 cup oats
- 1/3 cup all-purpose flour
- 1/3 cup brown sugar
- 1/4 cup melted butter

Procedure:

1. Preheat oven to 350°F (175°C). Grease a baking dish.
2. Rehydrate the strawberries by soaking them in water for about 20 minutes. Drain and place them in the baking dish. Sprinkle granulated sugar over the strawberries.
3. Mix oats, flour, brown sugar, and melted butter until crumbly. Sprinkle over strawberries.
4. Bake for 30-35 minutes or until the topping is golden brown.

Chocolate-Dipped Freeze-Dried Bananas:

Ingredients:

- 1 cup freeze-dried banana slices
- 1/2 cup chocolate chips (dark or milk chocolate)
- 1 tsp coconut oil

Procedure:

1. In a microwave-safe bowl, melt the chocolate chips with the coconut oil in 20-second intervals, stirring between each interval until smooth.
2. Dip each freeze-dried banana slice into the melted chocolate, ensuring it's coated on both sides.
3. Lay the dipped slices on a parchment-lined tray and let them harden in the refrigerator for about 20 minutes.

Berry Bliss Pudding:

Ingredients:

- 1 cup mixed freeze-dried berries (strawberries, blueberries, raspberries)
- 2 cups milk or dairy-alternative
- 1/4 cup chia seeds
- 2 tbsp honey or maple syrup
- 1 tsp vanilla extract

Procedure:

1. Rehydrate the mixed berries by soaking them in water for about 20 minutes. Drain.
2. In a bowl, mix together milk, chia seeds, honey, and vanilla extract.
3. Add the rehydrated berries to the mixture and stir.
4. Refrigerate for at least 4 hours, preferably overnight, until the pudding sets.

Freeze-Dried Mango and Coconut Parfait:

Ingredients:

-   1 cup freeze-dried mango slices
-   2 cups Greek yogurt
-   1/4 cup desiccated coconut
-   2 tbsp honey
-   Granola for layering

Procedure:

1. Rehydrate the mango slices by soaking them in water for about 20 minutes. Drain.
2. In a bowl, mix Greek yogurt with honey.
3. In serving glasses, layer yogurt, granola, rehydrated mango, and desiccated coconut. Repeat layers and top with a sprinkle of coconut.

Freeze-Dried Raspberry Chocolate Mousse:

Ingredients:

- 1 cup freeze-dried raspberries
- 3/4 cup heavy cream
- 4 oz dark chocolate (70% cocoa)
- 2 tbsp granulated sugar
- 1 tsp vanilla extract

Procedure:

1. Rehydrate the raspberries by soaking them in water for about 15 minutes. Drain and purée in a blender.
2. In a saucepan, melt the dark chocolate over low heat. Once melted, remove from heat and allow to cool slightly.
3. In a separate bowl, whip the heavy cream with sugar and vanilla until soft peaks form.
4. Gently fold the raspberry purée into the whipped cream, then fold in the melted chocolate until combined.
5. Divide the mousse among serving dishes and refrigerate for at least 2 hours before serving.

Tropical Freeze-Dried Fruit Bars:

Ingredients:

- 1 cup freeze-dried pineapple chunks
- 1/2 cup freeze-dried papaya pieces
- 1/4 cup freeze-dried kiwi slices
- 2 cups Greek yogurt
- 3 tbsp honey
- 1 tsp vanilla extract

Procedure:

1. Rehydrate the freeze-dried fruits by soaking them in water for 20 minutes. Drain.
2. In a bowl, mix the Greek yogurt with honey and vanilla.
3. Fold the rehydrated fruits into the yogurt mixture.
4. Pour the mixture into popsicle molds and freeze for at least 6 hours or until solid.

Freeze-Dried Blueberry Cheesecake Bites:

Ingredients:

- 1 cup freeze-dried blueberries
- 1 cup cream cheese, softened
- 1/2 cup powdered sugar
- 1 tsp vanilla extract

- 1/2 cup graham cracker crumbs

Procedure:

1. Rehydrate the blueberries by soaking them in water for 20 minutes. Drain.
2. In a mixing bowl, beat together the cream cheese, powdered sugar, and vanilla until smooth.
3. Gently fold in the rehydrated blueberries.
4. Scoop out teaspoon-sized amounts and roll into balls. Roll each ball in graham cracker crumbs.
5. Refrigerate for at least 2 hours before serving.

Caramelized Freeze-Dried Pear Tarts:

Ingredients:

- 1 cup freeze-dried pear slices
- 1/4 cup brown sugar
- 2 tbsp butter
- 1 pre-made pie crust (or homemade if preferred)
- 1 tsp ground cinnamon

Procedure:

1. Preheat oven to 375°F (190°C).
2. Rehydrate the pear slices by soaking them in water for 20 minutes. Drain.

3. In a skillet, melt the butter and add the brown sugar. Stir until dissolved. Add the rehydrated pear slices and cook until caramelized.

4. Roll out the pie crust and cut into small circles using a cookie cutter. Place each circle in a muffin tin.

5. Fill each pie crust with the caramelized pear mixture. Sprinkle with cinnamon.

6. Bake for 20-25 minutes or until the edges of the crust are golden. Allow to cool before serving.

Freeze-Dried Apple Pie Bites:

Ingredients:

- 1 cup freeze-dried apple slices
- 1/2 tsp ground cinnamon
- 1/4 tsp ground nutmeg
- 2 tbsp granulated sugar
- 1 pre-made pie crust
- 1 tbsp melted butter

Procedure:

1. Preheat oven to 375°F (190°C).

2. Rehydrate the apple slices by soaking them in water for 15 minutes. Drain and chop finely.

3. Mix the chopped apples with cinnamon, nutmeg, and sugar.

4. Roll out the pie crust and cut into small squares. Place a spoonful of the apple mixture in the center of each square.
5. Fold the squares over the apple filling to form triangles, pressing the edges with a fork to seal.
6. Brush each triangle with melted butter.
7. Bake for 15-18 minutes or until golden brown. Cool slightly before serving.

Pistachio and Freeze-Dried Cherry Clusters:

Ingredients:

- 1 cup freeze-dried cherries
- 1/2 cup roasted pistachios, chopped
- 10 oz white chocolate, melted

Procedure:

1. Rehydrate the cherries by soaking them in water for 15 minutes. Drain.
2. In a bowl, combine the rehydrated cherries and chopped pistachios.
3. Stir in the melted white chocolate until the fruit and nuts are well-coated.
4. Drop by spoonfuls onto a parchment paper-lined tray.
5. Refrigerate until set, about 30 minutes.

Freeze-Dried Peach Gelato:

Ingredients:

- 1 cup freeze-dried peaches
- 2 cups heavy cream
- 1 cup whole milk
- 3/4 cup granulated sugar
- 1 tsp vanilla extract

Procedure:

1. Rehydrate the peaches by soaking them in water for 20 minutes. Drain and blend into a smooth purée.
2. In a bowl, whisk together the peach purée, heavy cream, milk, sugar, and vanilla.
3. Pour the mixture into an ice cream maker and churn according to the manufacturer's instructions.
4. Transfer the gelato to an airtight container and freeze until firm, about 2 hours.

Chocolate and Raspberry Brownies:

Ingredients:

- 1/2 cup freeze-dried raspberries
- 8 oz dark chocolate, chopped
- 1/2 cup unsalted butter, melted

- 1 cup granulated sugar
- 2 large eggs
- 1 tsp vanilla extract
- 1/2 cup all-purpose flour
- 1/4 tsp salt

Procedure:

1. Preheat oven to 350°F (175°C). Grease an 8-inch square baking pan.
2. Rehydrate the raspberries by soaking them in water for 10 minutes. Drain.
3. In a bowl, melt the dark chocolate in the microwave in 20-second intervals, stirring after each interval.
4. Stir in the melted butter, sugar, eggs, and vanilla until smooth.
5. Fold in the flour, salt, and rehydrated raspberries.
6. Pour the batter into the prepared pan.
7. Bake for 25-30 minutes or until a toothpick inserted comes out with a few crumbs. Cool completely before cutting into squares.

Freeze-Dried Apricot Almond Tarts:

Ingredients:

- 1 cup freeze-dried apricots
- 1/4 cup almond butter

- 1/4 cup honey or maple syrup
- Pre-made mini tart shells (8-10 count)
- 1/4 cup slivered almonds, toasted
- Powdered sugar, for dusting

Procedure:

1. Rehydrate the apricots by soaking them in water for 15 minutes. Drain and chop finely.
2. In a bowl, mix together the almond butter and honey or maple syrup.
3. Fold in the chopped apricots.
4. Spoon the mixture into the pre-made tart shells.
5. Top with toasted slivered almonds.
6. Dust lightly with powdered sugar before serving.

Pineapple Upside-Down Cake:

Ingredients:

- 1 cup freeze-dried pineapple rings
- 1/4 cup unsalted butter, melted
- 1/2 cup brown sugar
- 1 1/2 cups all-purpose flour
- 2 tsp baking powder
- 1/2 tsp salt
- 1/2 cup unsalted butter, softened
- 1 cup granulated sugar

- 2 large eggs
- 1 tsp vanilla extract
- 1/2 cup milk

Procedure:

1. Preheat oven to 350°F (175°C).
2. Rehydrate the pineapple rings by soaking them in water for 20 minutes.
3. In a round cake pan, pour melted butter evenly, then sprinkle brown sugar over the butter. Arrange the rehydrated pineapple rings on top.
4. In a bowl, whisk together flour, baking powder, and salt.
5. In a separate bowl, cream together the softened butter and granulated sugar until light and fluffy. Beat in eggs one at a time, then stir in vanilla.
6. Gradually add the flour mixture to the wet ingredients, alternating with milk.
7. Pour batter over the pineapple rings in the cake pan.
8. Bake for 30-35 minutes or until a toothpick inserted in the center comes out clean.
9. Cool for 10 minutes in the pan, then invert onto a plate.

Blackberry Panna Cotta:

Ingredients:

- 1 cup freeze-dried blackberries
- 2 cups heavy cream
- 1/4 cup sugar
- 2 tsp unflavored gelatin
- 1/4 cup water
- 1 tsp vanilla extract

Procedure:

1. Rehydrate the blackberries by soaking them in water for 15 minutes. Drain and blend into a puree.
2. In a saucepan, heat the heavy cream and sugar until sugar dissolves but do not let it boil. Remove from heat.
3. Sprinkle the gelatin over the water in a small bowl and let stand for 5 minutes to soften.
4. Add the softened gelatin to the warm cream mixture and stir until dissolved.
5. Stir in the blackberry puree and vanilla.
6. Pour the mixture into dessert glasses or ramekins.
7. Refrigerate for at least 4 hours or until set.
8. Garnish with a few whole freeze-dried blackberries before serving.

Kiwi Sorbet:

Ingredients:

- 1 cup freeze-dried kiwi
- 1/4 cup sugar
- 2 cups water
- Mint leaves, for garnish

Procedure:

1. Rehydrate the kiwi by soaking them in water for about 10 minutes. Drain.
2. In a blender, blend the rehydrated kiwi, sugar, and water until smooth.
3. Pour the mixture into an ice cream maker and churn according to manufacturer's instructions.
4. Transfer to a freezer-safe container and freeze until solid.
5. Serve with mint leaves as garnish.

Passionfruit and Lime Cheesecake:

Ingredients:

- 1 cup freeze-dried passionfruit
- 1/2 cup sugar
- 1 tbsp lime zest
- 2 tbsp lime juice

- 2 cups cream cheese, softened
- 1/2 cup sour cream
- 1/4 cup powdered sugar
- Pre-made graham cracker crust

Procedure:

1. Rehydrate the passionfruit by soaking in water for 15 minutes. Drain.
2. In a blender, blend the rehydrated passionfruit, sugar, lime zest, and lime juice until smooth.
3. In a bowl, whip the cream cheese until smooth. Add the sour cream and powdered sugar, mixing until well combined.
4. Fold in the passionfruit and lime mixture.
5. Pour the filling into the pre-made graham cracker crust and refrigerate for at least 4 hours or until set.
6. Garnish with additional freeze-dried passionfruit and lime zest before serving.

Plum and Almond Galette:

Ingredients:

- 1 cup freeze-dried plums
- 1/4 cup sugar
- 1 tsp almond extract
- Pre-made pie dough

- 1/4 cup almond flakes
- 1 egg, beaten (for egg wash)
- Powdered sugar, for dusting

Procedure:

1. Preheat oven to 375°F (190°C).
2. Rehydrate the plums by soaking them in water for about 15 minutes. Drain and slice.
3. Toss the rehydrated plum slices with sugar and almond extract.
4. Roll out the pie dough into a rough circle and transfer to a baking sheet.
5. Place the plum mixture in the center of the dough, leaving a 2-inch border around the edge.
6. Fold the edges of the dough over the plums, pleating as you go.
7. Sprinkle almond flakes over the plums.
8. Brush the edges of the dough with the beaten egg.
9. Bake for 25-30 minutes or until the crust is golden.
10. Let cool slightly and dust with powdered sugar before serving.

Lychee and Rosewater Trifle:

Ingredients:

- 1 cup freeze-dried lychees
- 1/4 cup rosewater
- 1 cup whipped cream
- 1 cup sponge cake, cubed
- 1/4 cup pistachios, chopped

Procedure:

1. Rehydrate the lychees by soaking them in water mixed with rosewater for 10 minutes. Drain.
2. In individual glasses or a large trifle dish, layer the sponge cake cubes at the bottom.
3. Add a layer of rehydrated lychees.
4. Top with a layer of whipped cream.
5. Repeat the layers until all ingredients are used up.
6. Finish with a top layer of whipped cream and sprinkle with chopped pistachios.
7. Refrigerate for at least 2 hours before serving.

Kid-Friendly Freeze-Dried Delights

Banana Pancake Pops:

Ingredients:

- 1 cup freeze-dried bananas
- 1 cup pancake mix
- 3/4 cup milk
- 1 egg
- Chocolate syrup or maple syrup for dipping
- Wooden skewers

Procedure:

1. Rehydrate the freeze-dried bananas by soaking them in a little water for about 5 minutes. Drain and set aside.
2. In a bowl, mix together the pancake mix, milk, and egg until smooth. Fold in the rehydrated bananas.
3. Heat a non-stick skillet over medium heat.
4. Pour small, silver-dollar-sized pancakes onto the skillet.
5. Cook until bubbles form on top, then flip and cook the other side.
6. Once cooked, let the pancakes cool slightly. Stick wooden skewers into each pancake to make "pancake pops."
7. Serve with chocolate syrup or maple syrup for dipping.

Berry Yogurt Bites:

Ingredients:

- 1 cup freeze-dried mixed berries (strawberries, blueberries, raspberries)
- 2 cups Greek yogurt
- 2 tbsp honey

Procedure:

1. Crush the freeze-dried berries into a fine powder using a mortar and pestle or a blender.
2. In a bowl, mix together Greek yogurt and honey until well combined.
3. Gently fold in the berry powder until well incorporated.
4. Drop spoonfuls of the mixture onto a parchment-lined tray.
5. Freeze for at least 4 hours or until firm.
6. Serve as a refreshing and healthy snack!

Apple and Cinnamon Oat Bars:

Ingredients:

- 1 cup freeze-dried apples

- 2 cups rolled oats
- 1/4 cup honey
- 1/2 tsp cinnamon
- 1/4 cup almond butter (or any nut/seed butter)

Procedure:

1. Preheat the oven to 350°F (175°C).
2. Rehydrate the freeze-dried apples by soaking them in water for about 10 minutes. Drain and chop into small pieces.
3. In a large bowl, mix together the rolled oats, rehydrated apples, honey, cinnamon, and almond butter until well combined.
4. Press the mixture into a greased 8x8-inch baking pan.
5. Bake for 20 minutes or until golden brown.
6. Let it cool, then cut into bars and serve.

Tropical Fruit Smoothie:

Ingredients:

- 1/2 cup freeze-dried mango
- 1/2 cup freeze-dried pineapple
- 1 banana
- 2 cups milk or coconut milk
- 1 tbsp honey (optional)

Procedure:

1. Rehydrate the freeze-dried mango and pineapple by soaking them in water for about 10 minutes. Drain.
2. In a blender, combine the rehydrated mango, pineapple, banana, milk, and honey (if using).
3. Blend until smooth and creamy.
4. Pour into glasses and serve as a refreshing drink!

Fruit Roll-Ups:

Ingredients:

- 1 cup freeze-dried strawberries
- 1 cup freeze-dried raspberries
- 1/4 cup honey or agave syrup

Procedure:

1. Blend the freeze-dried strawberries and raspberries in a food processor until they become a fine powder.
2. Add honey or agave syrup and blend again until a smooth paste forms.
3. Spread the mixture thinly and evenly on a parchment-lined baking tray.
4. Place in a low-temperature oven (around 170°F or 75°C) or a dehydrator, allowing it to dry out slowly for about 6-8 hours.

5. Once dried, peel off the parchment paper, and cut into strips. Roll them up, and they're ready to eat!

Chocolate-Covered Grapes:

Ingredients:

- 1 cup freeze-dried grapes
- 1/2 cup dark or milk chocolate chips

Procedure:

1. In a microwave-safe bowl, melt the chocolate chips in 20-second intervals, stirring after each interval until smooth.
2. Dip the freeze-dried grapes into the melted chocolate, ensuring they are fully coated.
3. Place them on a parchment-lined tray and refrigerate until the chocolate sets.
4. Enjoy these delightful, crunchy, chocolatey treats!

Tropical Popsicles:

Ingredients:

- 1/2 cup freeze-dried pineapples
- 1/2 cup freeze-dried papayas
- 1 cup coconut water
- 1 tbsp agave syrup (optional)

Procedure:

1. Rehydrate the freeze-dried pineapples and papayas in a little water for about 10 minutes. Drain.
2. In a blender, mix the rehydrated fruits, coconut water, and agave syrup (if using) until smooth.
3. Pour the mixture into popsicle molds and freeze for at least 4 hours.
4. Once set, run the molds under warm water briefly to release the popsicles. Enjoy this refreshing treat!

Freeze-Dried PB&J Bites:

Ingredients:

- 1 cup freeze-dried strawberries or raspberries (for the jelly effect)
- 1/2 cup creamy peanut butter
- 1/4 cup honey
- 1 cup rolled oats

Procedure:

1. In a food processor, pulse the freeze-dried strawberries or raspberries until they form a fine powder.
2. In a bowl, mix together the peanut butter and honey. Add the berry powder and rolled oats, mixing until fully combined.
3. Roll the mixture into small bite-sized balls and place them on a parchment-lined tray.
4. Refrigerate for at least 2 hours before serving. These bites are a fun twist on the classic PB&J sandwich!

Chocolate Raspberry Truffles:

Ingredients:

- 1 cup freeze-dried raspberries
- 1/2 cup dark chocolate chips
- 1/4 cup heavy cream
- Cocoa powder for dusting

Procedure:

1. In a food processor, blend the freeze-dried raspberries into a fine powder.
2. In a separate bowl, melt the chocolate chips. You can do this in a microwave in 20-second intervals or using a double boiler.
3. Once melted, stir in the heavy cream until smooth, then fold in the raspberry powder.
4. Chill the mixture in the refrigerator for about 2 hours or until firm enough to handle.
5. Shape the mixture into small balls and roll them in cocoa powder.
6. Store in the refrigerator until serving. These truffles are a luxurious treat with a burst of raspberry flavor!

Understanding and Preparing for Varied Situations

Disaster Scenarios: Tailoring Food Storage for Specific Emergencies (Hurricanes, Earthquakes, Power Outages)

When considering food storage for emergencies, it's crucial to be aware of the specific requirements of different disaster scenarios. Not all emergencies are the same, and while there are general guidelines for emergency food storage, certain situations call for unique considerations. This section aims to provide insights into tailoring your food storage strategy to cater to specific emergencies such as hurricanes, earthquakes, and power outages.

- **Hurricanes:**
  - **Anticipation and Duration:** Unlike some other natural disasters, hurricanes usually come with a warning, allowing for last-minute preparations. However, the aftermath could leave one without power and essential services for days or even weeks.
  - **Food Storage Recommendations:** High on water content foods like freeze-dried fruits which can provide hydration. Salty snacks should be avoided due to increased thirst. Opt for whole meals that can be easily rehydrated with cold water. Ensure airtight and waterproof storage.

- **Earthquakes:**
    - **Anticipation and Duration:** Earthquakes strike without warning. Post-earthquake, there might be disruptions in regular services and power outages, but the duration of such disturbances can vary.
    - **Food Storage Recommendations:** Foods that require minimal preparation are ideal. Prioritize items that don't need water for rehydration, given that water sources might be compromised. Lightweight and portable food options are essential in case of evacuations.
- **Power Outages:**
    - **Anticipation and Duration:** These can occur without warning and can last from hours to several days, depending on the cause.
    - **Food Storage Recommendations:** Foods that don't require cooking or heating are ideal. Opt for meals and snacks that can be eaten right out of the package. Also, consider foods that can help maintain body temperature in colder climates.

Conclusion:

Regardless of the emergency type, a common thread is the need for long-lasting, nutrient-dense, and easily accessible food. While the above guidelines cater to specific disaster scenarios, it's always crucial to ensure a clean water supply, have a can opener if necessary, and rotate stored food regularly to keep it fresh and effective for your needs.

Long-term Storage

Planning for Extended Periods Without Access to Fresh Supplies

In an ever-changing world where uncertainties loom large, the importance of long-term food storage cannot be overstated. Whether you're prepping for natural disasters, economic downturns, or extended isolation periods, having a food supply that lasts is paramount. This section delves into the strategies and considerations for planning and maintaining food stores that can sustain for long durations without relying on fresh supplies.

- **Understanding the Basics:**
  - **Shelf Life:** The first step is understanding the expiration and best-by dates. Invest in foods

specifically prepared for long-term storage, often designed to last for years.

- o **Nutritional Value:** Stored food should provide essential nutrients. Look for foods fortified with vitamins and minerals to ensure a balanced diet even in isolation.
- **Packaging Matters:**
  - o **Moisture and Air:** These are enemies of long-term food storage. Opt for vacuum-sealed, moisture absorber-packed, and mylar-bagged products.
  - o **Light and Temperature:** Store food in a cool, dark place. Temperature fluctuations and exposure to light can degrade the quality and longevity of food.
- **Diversifying the Food Types:**
  - o **Grains and Legumes:** Staples like rice, wheat, beans, and lentils can last for years when stored properly. They provide essential carbohydrates and proteins.
  - o **Freeze-Dried and Dehydrated Foods:** These offer a variety of meal options, from fruits to complete entrees. Their low moisture content ensures longevity.
  - o **Canned Goods:** While heavier and bulkier, they can last for years and provide a variety of nutrients.

- **Water is Essential:**
  - **Water Storage:** For extended periods, ensure you have access to clean drinking water. Consider large storage containers and purification tablets.
  - **Water Consumption:** Remember that many dehydrated and freeze-dried foods require water to prepare. Factor this into your water storage plans.
- **Rotation is Key:**
  - **First In, First Out (FIFO):** Use older items first and replace them with newer stocks, ensuring freshness and reducing waste.
  - **Regular Checks:** Periodically inspect your food storage for signs of spoilage, pests, or package damage.
- **Consider Special Dietary Needs:**
  - **Allergies and Restrictions:** Ensure you store foods that everyone in your household can consume. This includes considering allergies, dietary restrictions, or medical conditions.
- **Conclusion:**
  While the idea of planning for extended periods without fresh supplies might seem daunting, a systematic and thoughtful approach can make it manageable and effective. Prioritize nutrition, diversify your food options, and ensure regular checks and rotations to maximize the benefits of long-term food storage.

Portable Kits: Creating Lightweight, Nutrient-Packed Survival Packs

In emergency situations, mobility can be a lifeline. Whether you're facing evacuation orders, planning a wilderness excursion, or prepping for unpredictable events, having a portable and lightweight survival food kit is essential. This chapter focuses on curating survival packs that are not only easy to carry but also packed with necessary nutrients to keep you energized and healthy.

- **Understanding the Basics of Portable Kits:**
    - **Purpose and Duration:** Determine the primary purpose of the kit (e.g., 72-hour emergency, week-long trek) to guide your food choices.
    - **Caloric Needs:** Estimate the daily caloric intake needed based on activity level, age, and other factors.
- **Selection Criteria for Portable Foods:**
    - **Weight:** Prioritize lightweight options like freeze-dried or dehydrated foods.
    - **Volume:** Consider the physical space foods will occupy in your pack. Vacuum-sealed items can be more compact.
    - **Preparation:** Opt for foods that require minimal preparation, especially those that don't need hot water or cooking.

- **Essential Components of a Survival Pack:**
    - ○ **Carbohydrates:** Lightweight options include oatmeal packets, rice cakes, and whole grain crackers.
    - ○ **Proteins:** Consider vacuum-sealed pouches of tuna or chicken, protein bars, and dehydrated legumes.
    - ○ **Fats:** Packets of nut butters, trail mix, or sealed pouches of olive oil can offer essential fatty acids.
    - ○ **Vitamins & Minerals:** Freeze-dried fruit and vegetable pouches can provide necessary micronutrients.
- **Hydration Solutions:**
    - ○ **Water Pouches:** While water is heavy, having a few emergency pouches can be life-saving.
    - ○ **Water Filtration and Purification:** Consider lightweight water filters or purification tablets for sourcing water on the go.
    - ○ **Electrolyte Tablets or Powders:** These can help replenish lost salts and minerals during strenuous activity or in hot conditions.
- **Special Dietary Considerations:**
    - ○ **Food Allergies and Intolerances:** Ensure you have alternatives available, such as gluten-free or nut-free options.
    - ○ **Children and Elderly:** They might have different nutritional needs or preferences, so consider including suitable food items.

- **Packing and Organization:**
  - **Durable Containers:** Use waterproof and rodent-proof containers to protect your food.
  - **Compartmentalization:** Organize foods by type or meal to make accessing them easier and more systematic.
  - **Expiration Dates:** Clearly mark expiration dates on the outside and rotate items as necessary.
- **Conclusion:**
  Creating a portable survival food kit requires thoughtful planning and selection. The goal is to ensure that, in times of need, you have a balanced diet that is both lightweight and nourishing. Regularly reviewing and updating your kit ensures that when the moment arises, you're prepared to sustain and thrive.

Reflecting on the Power and Promise of Freeze-Drying

Freeze-drying, or lyophilization, is more than just a preservation method; it's a bridge between modern technology and human survival instincts, ensuring nourishment even in the most challenging circumstances. As we conclude our exploration into the vast world of freeze-dried foods and survival scenarios, let's take a moment to reflect on the invaluable role that freeze-drying plays.

- **Preservation and Longevity:**
    - o The primary advantage of freeze-drying is the exceptional shelf-life it offers. Foods can remain edible and nutritious for years, ensuring that one is always prepared for unforeseen events.
- **Nutritional Integrity:**
    - o Freeze-drying retains the nutritional profile of foods. This ensures that, even in emergencies, one doesn't compromise on the essential vitamins, minerals, and other nutrients.
- **Weight and Portability:**
    - o By removing the moisture content, freeze-dried foods become incredibly lightweight, making them perfect for portable emergency kits, backpacking, and more.
- **Versatility and Variety:**
    - o From fruits to complete meals, the spectrum of freeze-dried foods is vast. This ensures that there's something for everyone, catering to different tastes and dietary restrictions.
- **Economic and Ecological Value:**
    - o Freeze-drying reduces food waste by extending the shelf life of perishables. Over time, this can lead to cost savings and reduced ecological impact.
- **Accessibility and Preparation:**
    - o In many survival situations, the ease of food preparation becomes crucial. Most freeze-dried foods only require water (which doesn't always

need to be hot) to be made ready for consumption.

Final Reflections:

In our rapidly changing world, where natural disasters, economic uncertainties, and global challenges seem to be on the rise, being prepared has never been more essential. Freeze-drying stands as a testament to human ingenuity, bridging the gap between preparation and necessity.

While no one can predict the future with certainty, armed with the knowledge and resources related to freeze-drying, you can face it with confidence. As we wrap up this guide, remember that the essence of survival is not just enduring but thriving. And with freeze-dried foods in your arsenal, thriving becomes a more attainable goal.

Encouraging Readers to Prepare and Be Resilient Using Lyophilized Foods

In the unpredictable landscape of life, there's a saying that rings true: "It's better to be prepared for an opportunity and not have one than to have an opportunity and not be prepared." This sentiment especially holds weight when discussing food security and emergency preparedness. Lyophilized (freeze-dried) foods offer a modern solution to age-old challenges. This chapter seeks to inspire and encourage readers to embrace this method as a means of fortifying resilience.

- **Understanding Resilience:**
    - o **Definition:** Resilience is the ability to bounce back from adverse situations, to adapt, and to continue forward.
    - o **The Role of Preparedness:** Preparation doesn't mean expecting the worst, but rather equipping oneself for various eventualities.
- **The Assurance of Freeze-Dried Foods:**
    - o **Consistent Availability:** Having a stash of lyophilized foods means always having access to nourishment, irrespective of external conditions.
    - o **Diverse Options:** From fruits and vegetables to hearty meals, the range of freeze-dried products ensures varied and enjoyable meals.
- **Emotional Comfort in Familiar Foods:**
    - o In stressful situations, familiar tastes can provide emotional comfort. With freeze-dried foods, you don't have to sacrifice your favorite dishes.
- **Economic Benefits:**
    - o **Cost-Efficiency Over Time:** Although the initial investment might be higher, the long shelf life of lyophilized foods can result in savings in the long run.
    - o **Reducing Food Waste:** By utilizing freeze-dried foods before they expire and replenishing your stash, you can minimize waste, making the most of your resources.

- **Community and Shared Preparedness:**
  - Encourage community preparedness by sharing knowledge and resources. A community that's prepared collectively stands a better chance in crises.
- **Educational Opportunities:**
  - **For Families:** Use the process of gathering and using freeze-dried foods as an educational moment for children, teaching them the importance of preparation and the science behind lyophilization.
  - **For Communities:** Offer workshops or informational sessions about emergency preparedness, emphasizing the role of lyophilized foods.
- **Final Thoughts:**

  Preparation, at its core, is an act of hope and foresight. By integrating lyophilized foods into your readiness plans, you're not just storing food — you're preserving peace of mind. Embracing this method is more than a practical choice; it's a step towards resilience, ensuring that no matter the challenges ahead, you and your community are fortified with sustenance, strength, and the spirit of endurance.